I0753552

" . . . ALL GATHERED ROUND ONE OL'-FASHIONED CHRIS'MAS DINNER!"

SONGS OF TWO CENTURIES

BY WILL CARLETON

AUTHOR OF "FARM BALLADS" "FARM FESTIVALS" "CITY LEGENDS"
"RHYMES OF OUR PLANET" ETC. ETC.

ILLUSTRATED

NEW YORK AND LONDON
HARPER AND BROTHERS, PUBLISHERS
1902

Published November, 1902.

To

THE MEMORY OF THE NINETEENTH

AND

THE SUCCESS OF THE TWENTIETH

PREFACE.

These poems were written partly in the Nineteenth and partly in the Twentieth Century: hence the name of the book.

It was a great privilege to live within the Nineteenth, with all its wonderful achievements. Few that had the privilege, could have wished that their lot had been cast in any other. It has been upon the whole the most wonderful world-drama of all, thus far.

The Twentieth Century has already made a fine beginning—largely as a continuation of the Nineteenth, but also with some achievements of its own. What it will do before it grows old, is a problem: but a problem full of hope.

If this book carries with it the spirit of the century not long past, and aids in some measure the aspirations of the one that is now upon us, its highest purpose will be accomplished.

C.

CONTENTS.

SONGS OF MONTHS AND DAYS:

PAGE

The Old Christmas Dinner 15
The Queen of the Days 17
Washington-Month 19
What Shall We Give? 20
Farmer Stebbins as Santa Claus 22
Exceptin' Tom 24
Arbutus 27
The Eclipse 28
Ancestors 31
In September 34
Farmer Stebbins at the Fair 35
A Contrast 38
The Thanksgiving Dance 39
Eagle and Turkey 42
Uncle Jake's Thanksgiving 43

Songs of Home Life:

	Page
Words that We could Understan'	47
As well as I.	51
Fixing the Clock	53
The Mocking-Bird	55
Up in the Loft	57
To a Dead Bird	59
The Two Boys	60
Blowing the Feather	62
Harvests	64
Stars of the Grasses	65
Good-by, Old Horse	66

Songs of the Rivers:

To Go A-Swimming	69
Where We Watered the Team	71
Chant of the St. Lawrence	72
The Oarsman's Story	75
Out of Alexandr' Bay	77
From Corn-field to River	79

Songs of the Mountains:

Prologue	83
To the Mountain Profile	85
To the Same	86
In the Mountains, you Know	88
Some Country Solace	90
The Maid of the Mountain	93

Songs of the Nation:

PAGE

Greater America ... 97
Song—Language of the Flag ... 99
Song—Westerland ... 100
New England's Home-Call ... 101
The March of the Volunteers ... 104
Do not Forget the Wounded ... 105
The Passing of the Mother ... 106
The Absent Soldier's Child ... 110
A Song for Our Fleets ... 112
Gridley ... 113
Comin' Back to 'Pelier ... 115
In the Wreckage of the Maine ... 117
Cuba to Columbia ... 118
Columbia to Cuba ... 120
Colloquy of Grief ... 122
A Man Has Died ... 124
The Victory-Wreck ... 125
Liberty's Torch ... 126

Songs of Pleasure and Pain:

Farmer Stebbins Awheel ... 131
The Funeral-Express ... 133
Took Johnnie to the Show ... 135
381 ... 137
To the Czar ... 139
To Fannie Crosby ... 142
The Maiden-Mother ... 144

PAGE

The Old Church-Bell 145

Monologue of Pain 147

Bicycle-Song 149

De Temperachewer 150

Always a "Kick" 152

The Convict and the Stars 153

NOTES: 155

ILLUSTRATIONS.

FACING PAGE

"*All gathered round one ol'-fashioned Chris'mas Dinner*" .... Frontispiece

"*They's Somethin' here that's wrong*" 52

"*Where we watered the Team*" 70

"*Where smile the clustered Landscapes*" 84

"*It was Morning 'mongst the Hill-tops*" 94

"*Our Iron Fleets, of grim and savage Beauty*" 112

"*Newest of Freedom's Daughters, my Help went out to Thee*" 120

"*Liberty's Radiance throwing over the Seas and the Lands*" 126

Songs of Months and Days.

THE OLD CHRISTMAS DINNER.

One ol'-fashioned Chris'mas dinner's wuth a dozen nowadays,
That delivered by instalments, in the sleek new-fangled ways.
Take me back, O almanac! to the time when sev'ral "courses"
Come together in a bunch, an' united all their forces!
'Twas a time when, j'ined together, old an' young an' saint an' sinner
Could be found all gathered round one ol'-fashioned Chris'mas dinner!
[Thus said Ahab Adams, merchant, from a stress of thought to free him,
To his brother Shubal Adams, who had come from Maine to see him.]

Oft I think that dinner over—how once more I'd like to try it!
But, you see, it can't be managed: all my money wouldn't buy it.
Can't fetch back the old-time frame-work; can't arrange the proper meetin':
Most of all the folks I'd ask there, long ago has quit their eatin'.

First I'd want a slice o' winter that would fetch out what was in you:
Air a haft o' glitterin' blades sharp as if they meant to skin you;
Froze-up cloud-boats near the hills, tryin' hard to make a landin',
Trees with snow-white blankets on, sleepin', like the hosses, standin';
Fences peakin' through the drifts, clear plate-glass across the river—
All the chimneys breathin' steam crawlin' upward with a shiver;
Sun a yellow chunk of ice—failed to furnish any heatin',
An' remains for nothin', 'cept to be present at the meetin';
Critters in the barn sharp-set as they was before you fed 'em;
Snow an' frost unusual sassy—yell out ev'ry time you tread 'em.
That would be a val'ble mornin', wuth the trouble of appr'isin'!
Glad that Chris'mas happened 'round, on a day so appetizin'!

Then I'd want our Dad on deck—up-an'-down as last year's cider—
Made us toe the mark, you know—but a fust-class good provider:
When he slung his banner out—"Come an' hev a Chris'mas dinner",
Ev'ry one that got the word knowed his stomach was a winner.
How they hus'led through the snow!—horses kep' their bells a-ringin',
Runners creakin' like a sign—gals a-cacklin' an' a-singin';

Ol' folks wrapped up double-bulk—baby-bundles half a dozen—
Dogs that wouldn't have thanked the dogs of the king to call 'em cousin!
So I'd hev 'em come an' come, ere the morning hour was through with;
Come in wagon-loads on runners—more than we knowed what to do with!

Mother—wouldn't I hev her there?—would I—well, somehow or other,
I hain't learned so I kin speak stiddy yet, concernin' Mother.
I see times that I would give half my days of growin' older,
For a half an hour of her, with her gray head on my shoulder.
[Thus said Ahab Adams, merchant, proud of his success, with reason,
And his good financial prospects growing brighter every season.]
When the folks was all set down, then, a proper need confessin',
I would hev Gran'father Jones ask a good ol'-fashioned blessin'.
Not a short, impatient one, such as often I hear muttered,
But a long one, that improved appetites while bein' uttered.
I would hev the vict'als there, on the start, as fur as able,
An' wouldn't dare to waste a prayer on a bare and empty table.
"Now, take hold an' help yourselves!" father'd say, with kind inflections;
An' the crowd that set around wouldn't need no more directions.

Though they all had journeyed far, ere the clock said half a minute,
Uncle Tom would make first base 'fore the others could begin it.
Uncle Jake could eat the most, through his ways discreet and subtle;
Aunt Melinda's knife would fly, swifter than a weaver's shuttle.
Cousin Ruth would pick her plate, every bit of food espyin';
Neighbor Spoon would very soon hev a wishbone up a-dryin'.
Cider-apple-sauce too strong would make Deacon Wilson hazy;
Cousin Sammy'd eat mince pie till he drove his mother crazy.
Forty others, more or less, caperin' round in Chris'mas clover,
Makin' friendships still more strong—healin' former fusses over;
Knives a-flashin', plates a-crashin', pewter spoons an' forks a-jinglin';
Ev'rything by chance contrived for to set your blood a-tinglin';
All as cozy as cud be, in a happiness bewild'rin';
Oh, if Christ could come in there, He'd hev said, "Keep at it, children!"

[Thus said merchant Ahab Adams, with rich presents to him clinging,
While in Christmas peals and chimes, all the city-bells were singing;
And he sank in thoughtful reverie—tried with all his might to guess
Why his joy was so much greater when his wealth was so much less;
How new splendors and rich banquets could not satisfy the inner
Soul and body, like the dear sweet old-fashioned Christmas dinner!]

THE QUEEN OF THE DAYS.

Now all of the days one day were met
  With sober and anxious mien,
To choose which one they owed the debt
  Of crowning it king or queen.

Then New Year shouted, "I always led
  The column, and always will;
Give me the crown for my gallant head!"
  But all of the days were still.

Then Easter spoke—the beautiful child—
  And told her gentle will;
They tenderly looked at her and smiled,
  But all of them yet were still.

Victoria's natal day was there,
  Hedged round with martial skill,
And a glorious reign without compare;
  But all of the days were still.

July had come with its ordnance-tone
  The world of the West to thrill;
And far was the birth of a nation known!
  But all of the days were still.

Thanksgiving lifted her thanks on high,
  And winsomely ate her fill;
The days looked up to the distant sky,
  But all of them yet were still.

Now Christmas came, divinely fair,
  Her eyes as a star-beam bright;

2

The gold of the sun was in her hair—
  Her form was a ray of light.

She held in the world's delighted gaze
  Good gifts for living and dead;
She smiled at all of her sister-days,
  But never a word she said.

All knew that the friendly strife was done,
  And never a word said they;
But knelt and crowned the beautiful one,
  As Queen for ever and aye.

WASHINGTON-MONTH.

February—February—
How your moods and actions vary,
　　Or to seek or shun.
Now a smile of sunlight lifting,
Now in chilly snowflakes drifting;
Now with icy shuttles creeping,
　　Silver webs are spun.
Now with laden torrents leaping,
　　Oceanward you run,
Now with bells you blithely sing,
　　'Neath the stars or sun;
Now a blade of murder bring
　　To the suff'ring one;
February—you are very
　　Dear, when all is done:
Many blessings rest above you;
You one day (and so we love you)
　　Gave us Washington.

WHAT SHALL WE GIVE?

What shall we give on a Christmas day?—
  Money?—they say it is sordid and old,
And hearts that are seeking the upward way,
  Are crushed to earth by the weight of gold.
And still does the bank-note's whisper bring
  The palace of pleasure yet more near;
And fair-faced coin, as together they ring,
  Are silver and golden bells of cheer.
So let not sentiment war with thrift;
But mingle them both, in a Christmas gift.

Give me a cluster of precious gems!
  Stars of the earth, that were born to rise
Into affection's diadems—
  Into the lover's changeful skies.—
Though all the jewels of rock and tide
  Should weave together in one strong ray,
'Twere nought but a burst of glow, beside
  The deathless glory of Christmas day!
Yet costly love is the earth-cloud's rift;
And gems are a goodly Christmas gift.

I see the broideries' colors flow
  Through palace-parlors and humble rooms:
Flit delicate fingers to and fro—
  The ivory shuttles of living looms.
Toil on at your queenly task, O queens!
  And wield your sceptres of form and hue;

The dainty fittings you give life's scenes,
  Will last eternity's drama through.
Earth's clouded curtains will fade and shift;
But loving toil is a deathless gift.

What shall we give on a Christmas day?—
  Whatever a heart to a heart can spare;
Whate'er through the dark can throw a ray—
  Whate'er can fetter the hands of care.—
Not all the riches of earth and sea
  Could build their statues one soul above;
And presents, if rightly weighed, must be
  Hung first on the golden scales of love.
While ever to Heaven our thanks uplift:
For God invented the Christmas gift.

FARMER STEBBINS AS SANTA CLAUS.

We went to Northtown visiting, my good old wife an' me,
An' thought that we would bathe ourselves in Chris'mas joy an' glee;
For Sarah Ann, a buxom dame, an' daughter, too, of mine,
Resides there with her older-half an' children eight or nine.
An' so we gathered gifts enough to make 'em all content,
An' took the train an' landed there the very day we went.

The children warmly greeted us an' crowded round my chair,
With four a-perchin' on my knees, an' young 'uns still to spare;
An' asked about my spectacles, an' how I growed my wig,
An' if my papa bought my teeth before I got so big;
An' how my whiskers come to bleach; an' other questions prone
To make a mortal realize that younger days have flown;

An' if I ever looked it up how far I was around,
An' when I run if it would shake the whole adjacent ground;
An' if the your-correct-weight box didn't think I was a lot,
An' if I wouldn't have to put two pennies in the slot;
With other questions well designed to give a hint to me
That I was not a first-class sylph, so far as they could see.

An' when I told 'em fairy-tales, they wouldn't believe a word,
An' said the Sin'bad sailor things could never have occurred;
An' all the pleasant little lies that used to cheer my youth
They set upon without delay as destitute of truth.
An' when of Christmas mysteries in solemn tones I spake,
They laughed an' said that Santa Claus was all "a bloomin' fake."

So Christmas eve I slyly told my daughter Sarah Ann:
"I'll show the tots a little sight to laugh at if they can.
You rake the fireplace clear o' fire, not tellin' them the cause,
An' I'll come down the chimney-way dressed-up as Santa Claus.
It isn't very fur to climb—the weather's pretty mild,
An' I would do three times as much to interest a child."

I went an' clad in hairy garb, with whiskers long an' white,
An' other things to paralyze the inexperienced sight,
An' had some sleigh-bells bright an' new a hangin' on my arms,
An' pockets full o' Christmas things to add unto my charms;
An' with the strongest ladder-rope that I could find in town,
I entered in the chimney-top an' clambered slowly down.

My goodness sakes! Whoever heard of such untimely luck?
The chimney narrowed all at once, an' suddenly I stuck!
An' hung there like a roastin' hen a-waitin' to be brown,
For spite of all my effortin' I couldn't get up or down.
An' then the chil'ren heard the noise and run distressin' fleet,
An' looked and yelled: "It's Gran'pa Steb: we know him by his feet!"

An' then their mother had to tell what I had tried to do,
Whereat their little fancies sprung the subject to pursue:
They asked me if I'd traveled far, if chimneys injured coats,
An' where my span of reindeers was, an' if they'd like some oats;
An' told me, with a childish greed for Christmas-gathered pelf,
If I would throw the presents down, I needn't come myself;

An' there I hung for quite a while, with fury in my heart,
Until they brought a mason in, who took the bricks apart;
An' though they made the children stop an' sent 'em off to bed,
I knowed what they was thinkin' of, an' what they prob'ly said.
An' when the mornin' light appeared, an' breakfast-time occurred,
They sat around the table there forbid to say a word;

A-sufferin' so to laugh at me, afraid that I'd be gruff,
An' longin' for their presents, too—I knowed it well enough.
An' then a tear come in my eye, an' like a fond old dunce
I went an' dug the presents out an' give 'em all to once.
An' then I says, "If Santa Claus is what you call 'a fake',
These pretty things he brought fur you is real an' no mistake."

An' then they up an' danced around an' kissed me, one by one,
An' hugged me harder than the blamed old chimney just had done,
An' with a thousand looks of love incumbered me with thanks,
An' made me like 'em more an' more in spite of all their pranks;
An' one, the prettiest of the whole, who always took my part,
She smiles an' says: "It's Gran'pa Steb: we know him by his heart!"

EXCEPTIN' TOM.

'Twas on a cloudy winter day,
  An' snow was gently fallin',
When Tom an' I upon the sleigh
  A heavy load was haulin';
We was committee—him an' me—
To find the annual Christmas-tree
  (With thanks for all our toil an' search),
  To deck the Presbyterian church.

It wasn't any little shrub
  With which we two was dealin'—
We knowed the top would almos' rub
  The meetin'-house's ceilin';
Two yoke of oxen drawed in line,
An' one was Tom's an' one was mine;
  An' trudgin' 'long, we fell, we two,
  A-gossipin' like women do.

We done our own longcomin's brown,
  An' other people's knavery;
We talked of all the girls in town,
  Not countin' Gretchen Avery.
We wasn't on speakin' terms that day
Regardin' her, as one might say;
  She had two would-be beaux, you see,
  An' one was Tom an' one was me.

But Tom he acted over-bright
  For one with even chances;
An' hinted of the past delight
  Of parin'-bees an' dances;
And how some one a gift would get
To drive 'em farther into debt;
  An' other little hints, in jerks,
  That started up my thinkin'-works.

The tree was taller still that night,
  As if't had been a-growin',
With presents on it fair an' bright
  An' candles near 'em glowin',
And all the folks for miles aroun'
Had brought their presents into town:
  The tree bore all things, sweet an' sour,
  From candy-sticks to bags of flour.

An' Tom an' I each other sought,
  Bein' fellow-men in slavery;
But he, the sly, a gift had brought,
  To hang for Gretchen Avery.
'Twas somethin' in the jewel line—
I watched him peek, and saw it shine;
  He gave a switchin' look at me
  An' went an' put it on the tree.

An' then I says: "I won't be beat
  In cunnin' or in bravery!"
An' so I went an' sought a seat
  Adjoinin' Gretchen Avery.
An' she was rather kind, for her—
More like a sister, as it were;
  An' fluttered some'at from her perch,
  There in the Presbyterian church.

She asked me all about the tree,
  An' where I found it growin';
An' whispered, thanks was due to me,
  For such a boon bestowin';

But I was minded to be fair,
An' spoke her honest, then an' there:
"Tom is the man for you to see:
He worked four times as hard as me."

An' then she glanced at Thomas, near,
An' smiled unduly pleasant;
An' then I spoke up: "Say, see here:
Suppose one gets a present
On yonder tree, as well they may—
Then shouldn't they take it, anyway?"
An' quick at me the words she thrust:
"How can you ask? Of course they must!"

So when they all marched round, you see,
Their gifts to be a-fetchin',
I gave a jump into the tree,
Right there in front of Gretchen:
An' words was nowhere near my tongue,
But on my arm a motto hung:
"This is a present, all can see,
To Gretchen Avery—made by me."

Now wasn't she a han'some show,
To all the people gazin'?
An' now she looked like drifted snow,
An' then like sunsets blazin';
Then like a queen she stood up there,
An' never flinched or flecked a hair;
But sweetly said to Elder Brown:
"Please kindly hand my present down?"

An' goin' home, she says to me,
In tones that still is haunted:
"I think tonight that all I see
Got just the gift they wanted."
And I didn't say much in our walk,
Not bein' strong upon the talk;
But couldn't sift my feelings from
The pityin' words: "Exceptin' Tom!"

ARBUTUS.

Under the snow, under the snow,
The leaves of the trailing arbutus grow;
Toiling the earth that loves them nigh,
But hoping to some day see the sky.

Under the snow, under the snow,
The flowers of the trailing arbutus glow;
E'en in the dark their duty done,
But hoping to some day kiss the sun.

THE ECLIPSE.

May 28, 1900.

A gleaming sun, well hoisted up the sky.
Round as when Ossian sang his feeble praise,
Bright as when Joshua gave it word to halt;
Waiting to be o'ershadowed by the moon—
Meek planetette—dog of the humble earth.
Waiting?—no: *we* were waiting: what to him
If for an hour some few rays were flung back
From the chilled world? 'Twas not Earth's ruling star,
But we—that waited: we who long decades
Had watched for him to vanish in mid-day,
That we might scan the comrades that he kept,
And trace rare secrets, darkened by his light.
'Twas we that waited—once again to know
If figures, called from long and wakeful nights,
That had for generations an event
For this great hour forewarned—told truths or lied.

The grass-lawn stretched to greet a southern sky,
By verdant trees eclipsed; the scolding birds
Threw agile shadows on the tossing grain;
A cloud, far in the deep mysterious west,
Darkened another cloud; the constant stars
Were covered by the flaming light of morn;
The city, half a hundred miles away,
That glared at us last eve through all that space,
With home-made lightnings—distance now obscured.

The great sun went about his daily task,
As ever in the death-darked centuries
That shrink in History's coffin. Not far off
He smiled at grave-stones—each a marble groan—
Voicing the sad and helpless grief of man,

That life must ever be eclipsed by death.
He seemed to smile that Earth, which night on night
Throws its own self in shadow—now should prate
At shadow of the moon.

Oh, not alone
We stood upon the breezy verdant hill,
And hailed the high event: a million eyes—
Ten million eyes—made journey with our own
Unto the burning globe: from hill and plain—
From field and palace—souls were traveling
To yonder soul of planets.

Lofty minds
That hunger always for the infinite,
Had a most godly feast; ignoble eyes
Looked at the sky for once; life's vaudeville
Viewed a rare act—a solemn pantomime
Billed for a century; superstition crouched
In haunts of mingled terror and delight,
Half doubting and half fearing.

Ah! just now
A tiny gold-clad sentry of Time's camp
With slender finger points the magic hour
That generations could not wait to see:
The breathless instant is not far away.

'Tis here! It fastens to the sun's sharp edge
And leads its many black-draped followers on:
The dragon that Columbus one dread day
Discovered while the savages knelt low
And made of him a god, is here again;
And slowly creeps the shadow.

Down, and down,
It delves, into the gold-mine of the sky.
Our sun is but a fragment of a sphere;
And now a crescent; 'tis a new new-moon
Brighter than any that we e'er have seen,

Greets our right shoulder!—Now—there is no sun—
No moon.

The green-tipped pines upon the lawn
Have gathered dusk, and sung a twilight song;
The birds fly home and nestle 'mid their leaves;
Through this new night the cattle now begin
Their stated pilgrimage from field to fold;
Brave steeds fling out their nostrils in affright;
And e'en the stars seem puzzled; for, just now,
The coy and wayward Mercury peeps down,
Now first for many years by day unveiled;
And comes a gleam from old Orion's belt.

Night has come back, that but a few short hours
Left us as ever: what had she forgot—
Dear, dreamy Night?

The morning walks in black;
The air grows chill; a weirdness is abroad;
'Tis like a fragment of the great last hour;
And well a mind not tutored by the voice
Of God-given Science, might fall dead with fright.

But look!—once more a crescent!—light again
Is victor in this battle of the sky!
Broader and broader grows the curve of gold—
Deeper and deeper nestles gloom in gloom—
And now at once the welcome sun again
Illumines earth, and sends a message down:

"This sunset and this sunrise in mid-sky,
Both in the hour—are signals that may mean—
If man so long such wonders can foresee—
What cannot God? If He can dim the sun
With worlds for clouds, and sweep them off again,
Can He not wipe away your clinging tears,
And move the fragile clouds 'neath which you walk,
O children of His heart?"

ANCESTORS.

We went to the Fourth of July—
Marjorie—she an' I—
Where drums was beaten, an' chickens eaten,
An' banners floated high;
An' though I hoped she would some time love me,
Still I felt that she felt above me;
(I was awkward, an' hung my head,
An' she was a reg'lar thoroughbred.)

Marjorie, by the by,
Had more ancestors than I;
She had a knack of goin' back
Along in History's covered track,
An' pickin' her great-grandfathers out,
An' stan'in' 'em up to be bragged about.
She had a book of 'em, all in rows,
Some several thousan', I suppose;
One was a colonel, an' one a squire,
An' one was a king, or somethin' higher;
There were three brothers on fortune-hunts,
That all come over the sea at once;
An' some of 'em, by the by,
Helped make the Fourth of July;
But though their acts she couldn't condemn,
She hadn't much time to dwell on them,
But sailed her gallant ancestral bark
Almost in hailin' of Noah's ark!
An' I—poor I—

Hadn't nothin' much to reply,
Excep' that gran'father had fine ways,
An' played the bugle on trainin' days.

Marjorie, han'some an' high
(I loved her, by the by),
Enjoyed the day in a sight-seein' way,
An' so, for a time did I.
But we found, on the picnic ground,
A chap from some other village we knew,
An' he had a pedigree-weakness, too;
They learned, that a thousan' years ago,
They was relations, or nearly so;
An', standin' there by a maple tree,
Talkin' about their pedigree,
They went a-wanderin', hand in hand,
(Speakin' in figures) by sea an' land;
An' I hadn't much to say that was fine,
Excep' that a great-great-uncle of mine
Was (in the Methodist Church, you know,)
Presidin' elder, some years ago.

So feelin' sort of alone, you see,
An' terrible short of pedigree,
But never carin' to mope around
If any cheerfulness could be found,
I visited gaily, with smiles to spare,
The secon'-prettiest maiden there.
An' she, though cozy an' sweet an' fine,
Didn't hang on any ancestral line,
An' had no forebears to be thankful for,
Exceptin' one in the Blackhawk war.
There on the Fourth of July,
This secon'-best girl an' I,
We was a-talkin', gay's could be,
When Marjorie come right up to me,
With manners that caused me some surprise,
An' shadows of tears in her great black eyes;
An' "will you kindly go with me,
And help me find my mother?" said she.

An' off we went—the finest of girls,
Bearin' the blood of a dozen earls,
An' I with none, as one might say,
Exceptin' what I had brought that day.
We left the young man by the tree,
Standin' alone with his pedigree;
While the gal I'd talked to, again began
A-makin' eyes at her best young man.

Marjorie drew a sigh,
There on the Fourth of July,
An' made no bother to find her mother,
Her mother, proud an' high,
An' always a-hangin' nigh;
But walked an' walked an' hung her head,
An' "Why are you hateful to me?" she said:
"I couldn't be hateful", says I,
"To one that I've loved five years or more,
An' never dared to tell it before,
Because she was born in the lap of fame,
An' I hadn't an ancestor to my name."
She walked a little closer to me:
"I've got enough for us both", says she:
An' looked as if she would cry,
There on the Fourth of July.

IN SEPTEMBER.

The Summer seems pausing a moment for rest,
In September;
The Autumn is watching her out of the west,
And soon he will come in his fire-dappled vest.
But how like a mourner the forests will wail,
And how on the meadows will rattle the hail,
In November!

With clusters of beauty the vines are aglow,
In September;
How sweetly and softly the zephyrs can blow,
How wed to the sunlight the streamlets that flow!
But all of a sudden a chill in the air
Creeps up like a spirit, and whispers "Prepare
For December!"

FARMER STEBBINS AT THE FAIR.

They brought the biggest oxen that you ever ever see,
They fed 'em an' they combed 'em in a manner new to me;
They stood 'em up together like a row of checker-corns,
Fur to play a game o' primiums fur some ribbins on their horns.
  Mac was there, an' Jack was there,
  Si was there, an' I was there,
An' vowed that bulls of Bashan, or of any town or nation,
Couldn't match us what was doin' in the bellowin' an' the mooin',
  That was floatin' through the air, at the Cobb County Fair.

They brought the biggest roosters that had ever ever crowed,
An' the hens that cackled loudest when you met 'em in the road,
An' the butter that is yellerest when you yank it from the churn,
An' the cheese that when you bite it gives your mouth the most concern.
  Sal was there, her gal was there,
  An' Lu was there, an' Sue was there,
  Fan was there, an' Ann was there,
An' the Sarys an' the Marys, with selections from their dairies,
While of eggs the finest pickin's—Natur's vain attempts at chickens,
  There was plenty an' to spare, at the Cobb County Fair.

They brought the sleekest hosses that we'd ever sighted yet,
An' they trotted 'em an' run 'em, an' forbid the folks to bet;
As is oft in human natur', in that case it did befall
That the one we tuk fur smartest was the slowest of 'em all.
  'Than, he guessed, an' Dan, he guessed,
  An' Sim computed, an' Jim computed,

An' Lo, he wagered, an' Jo, he wagered,
U-*ry* bet, an' I bet;
An' 'twan't what you'd be seekin' in a church-trustee or deakin;
An' we didn't do any winnin' that was big enough fur sinnin';
But we couldn't take a dare, at the Cobb County Fair.

They got a pig an' greased it, though I think 'twould run without,
An' whoever grabbed an' held it, 'twould be his, beyond a doubt.
So we neighbors 'greed to try it, jest to show what we could do,
An' to salt it in our barrels fur to help the winter through.
Smalley grabbed it, an' Hawley grabbed it,
An' Whaley missed it, an' Bailey missed it,
Lafe Calkins clutched it, Sam Hawkins clutched it,
Abe Maxson fell over it, Frank Jackson fell over it,
Jim Fry rolled under it, an' I rolled under it;
But it shifted its position sleek as any polertician,
An' where'er we flung our mettle, there the grease appeared to settle;
So we suffered wear an' tear, at the Cobb County Fair.

There come the finest maidens you would notice any day,
An' I didn't take the trouble fur to look the other way:
E'en a nettle or a thistle, if possessed of human power,
Wouldn't turn their eyes a minute from a sweet an' bloomin' flower.
Taller gals an' smaller gals,
Comely gals an' humly gals,
Giddy gals an stiddy gals,
Gold-made gals an' old maid gals,
Blue-eyed gals an' true-eyed gals,
Spread-haired gals an' red-haired gals—
All a-losin' of their mothers, an' a-goin' round with others,
Walkin', runnin', flirtin', dancin', an' invar'ably entrancin':
'Twas excitement to be there at the Cobb County Fair.

I took some fall pippins big as ever tempted Eve,
An' they tempted everybody that beheld 'em, I believe:
No, the jedges didn't jedge 'em, an' they've never jedged 'em yet:
For before they come acrost 'em, ev'ry single one was e't!
Lon e't 'em, an' John e't 'em,
An' Grace e't 'em, an' Ace e't 'em,

An' Horner e't 'em, an' Warner e't 'em,
Old Phœbe e't 'em, Bill Beebe e't 'em,
The Ryans e't 'em, th' O'Briens e't 'em,
The Sloanses e't 'em, the Joneses e't 'em,
Tom Griggs e't 'em, an' the pigs e't em:
There was ev'rybody chankin' without e'en a sign of thankin';
An' I driv home a-rippin', 'thout a primium or a pippin;
An' a mighty little share of the Cobb County Fair.

A CONTRAST.

October held a carnival,
    When Summer days had fled;
His halls were trimmed with blue and gold,
    And banners flaming red.
Now all the world with fowl and fruit
    Were at his table fed;
The richest wine of bough or vine
    Before his guests was spread.

October held a funeral,
    When Summer nights were fled;
And all the leaves and all the vines
    And all the flowers were dead.
The richly colored drapery
    Was burial robes instead,
And shorn of pride, he lay and died
    Upon a humble bed.

THE THANKSGIVING DANCE.

Wall, November's on us now—such as up to date is livin'—
An' it won't be many sunsets 'fore we've got a new Thanksgivin'.
Mebby with ungrateful heart an' a prayin' mouth to screen it:
Sometimes form is better'n nothin'—even when they do not mean it.
[Thus said Ahab Adams, merchant, quiet 'mid the city's Babel,
Lounging in his inner office, while his feet adorned a table.]

Well, we boys looked forward fur it—used to long to give it greetin'—
Half the day inside a pew—half a-guzzlin' an' a-eatin'.
We was then ungrateful scamps—all religious joys a-shirkin';
But we yelled fur any minute that would let us loose from workin'.
Most of us is lab'rers now—with our feelin's much amended;
Fur we're maybe at the work that the Lord fur us intended!
[Then he hugged his elder brother, with a motion kind but bearish:
He was the devoted pastor of a first-class city-parish.]

Yes, we mostly liked Thanksgivin', or the day we used to call so,
When we used to eat an' eat till the stomach-ache came also!
But the best one I remember was, most ev'ry hour an' minute,
One Thanksgivin'-party with no Thanksgivin'-dinner in it!

Recollect in '53? how the crops come in, that season!
Everything bobbed up as ef it possessed some special reason;
Corn-ears looked like clubs of gold—wheat made faces at the measure;
Oats an' rye an' punkin vines seemed as if they growed for pleasure.

Round-eyed grape-stems 'twas a joy even just to hev a sight of;
Apples mebby like the one Eve went wrong to get a bite of.
An' I recollect you said, as you dug a two-pound tater,
"Ef there's anything that's failed, surely 'tisn't old Mammy Natur!"

Then, to make the whole concern more entrancin' an' delightin',
Nations far across the sea fell to bickerin' an' to fightin';
Killed each other for the sake of their boundaries enlargin';
An' we Yankees hed to feed 'em—an' we didn't forgit the chargin'.
After all the lean lank years, now hed come a fine an' fat one;
An' we capered round as ef all the rest would be like that one.
So we said, "There's fun ahead": our hard days' works we would sof'n
With a dinner in our minds such as didn't come very of'n.

But there's one thing you can bank on: earthly joys is few an' fleetin':
Dad and Mam went off that week to a 'Sociation'l meetin'!

Well, seven brothers in one house, with no women-folks to aid 'em
Couldn't make vict'als utter thanks—though we worked hard to persuade 'em:
Flour an' dough for us wouldn't go; fire had ruther roast our fingers;
Gracious! how that cookin'-bee in the mem'ry lurks an' lingers!
So we dumped into a ditch all our culinary labors;
An' you says, "Le's hev a shindig an' invite the nearest neighbors!"

Gracious! how we took the word 'mong the misters, maids, an' madams,
"There will be a dance tonight at the house of Deacon Adams!"
What surprise was in all eyes; how with questions they would work us!
'Twouldn't hev rattled folks much more ef we'd hed a three-ring circus.
But they come at candle-lightin'—scores of 'em with curious greetin';
First time Deacon Adams' house ever hed that sort of meetin'!

Cross-eyed Baker worked the fiddle: though no sweet professional beauty,
Couldn't he make a dancin'-tune skip aroun' an' do its duty?
Wasn't his head chock full o' notes! yellin', moanin', cooin', glancin'—
Ef he'd tried, I almost think he could set a graveyard dancin'!
Broke one string, the first dumbed thing; but he rose to that superior
In a way that made our cat tremble fur its own interior!
What a voice he hed, besides!—half a roar an' half a ripple:
He could "call off" in a way that would give legs to a cripple.

Not a dance he undertook, but he made us all go through it;
Folks went trippin' 'mongst the figgers that I never thought could do it.
People that was sick abed when they got the invertation,
Now was with us in the shindig, dancin', too, like all creation;
Skippin' o'er the hard-wood floor—all its cracks an' j'ints an' hummocks—
Givin' thanks there with their heels, ef they couldn't with their stomachs.

Recollect old Nathan Davis?—how he made the windows rattle!
Couldn't hev caused a bigger racket ef he'd brought a drove of cattle!
Recollect Cordelia Close, of the spinsterette pursuasion?
Little thing hadn't danced before, maybe, sence the Dutch invasion.
Recollect Lycurgus Straw?—local preacher, full o' feelin':
Looked on: said he didn't think it was half as bad as stealin';
Recollect old Gran'pa Purdy?—worked up by that fiddle's mockin's,
He jest jerked off both his boots, prancin' roun' in white-toed stockin's;
Oh, I tell ye it was fine! full o' music joy an' clatter!
Not a morsel fur to eat, but a pile to make us fatter!

An' when everything was gorgeous, an' our blood was still a-heatin',
Dad an' Mam come happenin' in—unexpected home from meetin'.

EAGLE AND TURKEY.

The eagle o'er us sweeping
Hath empires in his keeping;
From mountain-summits leaping,
    He swims the liquid sky;
Great cannon hoarsely falling
On timid ears appalling,
To him are brothers calling,
    The Fourth day of July.

But when the Autumns gather
Their leaden-golden weather,
And camp in woods and heather
    'Mid waves of gleaming fire,
When mortals are redressing
Past errors by confessing
A year's undoubted blessing—
    The eagle must retire.

As round the table teeming
With goodly victual steaming,
Each fragrant dish is seeming
    To thank Heaven all it can,
When every plate is pensioned
With morsels prayer-intentioned,
No eagle e'er is mentioned:
    The turkey leads the van.

UNCLE JAKE'S THANKSGIVING.

There's a lot o' folks they say that's a-holdin' up today
  Several mercies that they only just have found;
There's a river full o' thanks that's a-bustin' of its banks,
  An' a-inundatin' all de country round.

Dar's a lot o' folks I fear that's attracted by de cheer,
  An' is thankin' like dey never thanked before;
An' there's lots o' fervent pra'rs like de tickets on de cars—
  Good fur dis yer one day only an' no more.

I'm a-going to make dis day sort of up an' cl'r de way
  Fur a reg-lar thank-procession thro' de yeah;
So I'll sort o' set me down 'fore de odder folks is roun',
  An'll undertake to view my mercies cleah.

Here's dis rheumatis': I s'pose it's a blessin' in repose,
  Fur I'm happy when it isn't to be foun';
Must've ketched it from de moon in de season of de coon;
  An' I s'pose o' co'se de Lawd was watchin' roun'.

Here's dis bullet in my knee; 'twan't by no request o' me,
  But it cured me from de nights I used to roam;
An' I think in that affair, dat de Lawd was surely there;
  Fur I'm raisin' all my chickens now to home.

My ten chil'ren I suppose good as offspring gen'lly goes,
  But deir everlastin' tricks won't let me be;
All de fool'ry I concealed, in deir actions is revealed;
  An' dat's whar de Lawd has got a joke on me.

Dese yer enemies I've got, can be 'stroyed as well as not,
  Ef I only count de whole mankin' as fren's;
An' de stabs an' jabs dey gib underneath de lower rib,
  Is chastisin' dat de Lawd A'mighty sen's.

When dere comes a melon-famine, an' de vines is all a-shammin',
  It's intended I wid gratitude should think
Of de seasons furder back, when dere wasn't any lack
  Of dat hebbenly fruit containin' food an' drink.

An' de dollars I done see dat didn't even call on me,
  An' de less or greater loved ones dat I've lost—
All de t'ings dat I'm bereft, makes me thankful fur what's left;
  An' is worth to soul an' body all dey cost.

An' a million joys dar are, from de daisy to de star,
  Dat is worth de time of countin' o'er and o'er;
But of all thank-timber yet, it's the things I *didn't get*,
  That I think I hev to be de thankfulest for.

Songs of Home Life.

WORDS THAT WE COULD UNDERSTAN'.

Johnny left the farm, an' studied
  In the college, quite awhile;
He was sort of student-blooded,
  With a dash o' city-style;
So we talked it—me an' Father—
An' concluded we would rather
  Toil an extra hour or two
Every day, than let work gall him
  That he wasn't built to do;
An' where Nature seemed to call him,
  He should go; an' if a dollar
Now an' then, the Fates would bribe
  To produce a first-class scholar
For to tassel off our tribe,
We would take it out in knowledge;
So we put the boy to college.

Johnny lots o' letters sent us,
  Full o' things we knowed before,
An' a heap o' trouble lent us
  Studyin' of 'em o'er and o'er;
While his keep we kep' on earnin'
  From our hard an' sulky lan',
We was 'fraid he couldn't be learnin'
  Much, if writin' with school-han'
Words that *we* could understan';
An' we worried much about him
An' begun to fear an' doubt him.

An' I says one day to Father,
  "I'm a-goin' to put a stay

To this everlastin' bother:
  I shall start for John today."
An' Pa said, with mannish guesses
  'Bout a woman's clothin'-life,
"You are ruther short o' dresses
  Fur to go to college, Wife.
Not in *length* of any of 'em,
  But in *number's,* what I mean."
An' I says, "I'll rise above 'em,
  For I'm al'ays neat an' clean;
  An' I'll wear my bombazine,
With substantial hooks an' eyes,
An' the sleeves a Christian size."
An' I done jus' as I say,
An' went off that very day.

Well, I got there one fine mornin',
An' without a second's warnin',
I, his mother, an' no other—
His own true, hard-workin' mother,
Who had teached the boy to walk,
An' not only that, but talk:
(An' I said, "His eddication
  With them things left out, I guess,
Would hev been a tribilation,
  Nothin' more an' somethin' less")
I went hither, there, an' yon,
Jest inquirin' after John.

An' I traced him here an' there,
  An' kep' jest so fur behind him,
But somehow, I do declare,
  I could never seem to find him!
An' I thought, in great distress,
"He is dodgin' me, I guess:
Me, an' my old faded dress!"

Then my heart made sad complaint,
An' I felt homesick an' faint;
My appearance I compared

With some ladies' that was passin',
An' reflected, while they stared
At my scrimped-up way of dressin';
An' how my old bombazine
Looked so shabby-like an' mean.
An' I thought, with eyes tear-dim,
"Our sweet boy, that used to love us,
We have eddicated him—
Eddicated him above us!"

An' while these thoughts I was summin',
An' was kind o' prone to fear him,
I looked up an' saw John comin'
With a lady some'at near him!
Then I said, "It sha'n't be said
That I ever yet have stood
With a downcast, shamefaced head,
Front of my own flesh an' blood;
An' I teached the boy to talk,
An' not only that, but walk."
An' I says, "His conversation
With that purty gal I see,
Wouldn't hev proved much consolation
Ef it hadn't hev been fur me."
So I hurried proudly on,
With such courage as I'd got,
In a sort o' way that John
He c'u'd notice me or not.

When jest opposite, he turned,
An' he see my faded dress—
An' his fair face quickly burned,
With some small ashamèdness;
An' no wonder; for, you see,
There was her, trim as could be,
Dressed like pictur's on the wall,
An' life's sweetness through it all—
For a han'some gal was she!
An' just six foot off was me—
Wrinkled—old—though spick an' clean,

Dressed in my ol' bombazine,
An' with han's as hard as leather
(Me an' Dad oft worked together).
An' my throat was in one lump,
An' my heart it took a jump;
An' I hed all I could do
Holdin' back my feelin's, too;
For ol' times I couldn't forget;
An' I loved him—loved him yet—
Just as well, it should be stated,
As 'fore he was eddicated;

"But", I says, "I'll walk right on:
 I will curb my feelin's so
 His nice gal shall never know
That I'm any kin to John."

Walk right on!—it couldn't be done,
 With John's heart there in the road
 Bigger than a barley-load!
He went fur me on a run,
An' he kissed my wrinkled cheek,
 An' my hands so hard an' rough,
An' wouldn't sca'cely let me speak,
 Though I tried to, times enough;
An' half led, half carried me
As if proud as proud could be,
Up to where she stood; an' said,
"It's my mother"; an' her head
Bent as willer trees will do,
An' she hugged an' kissed me, too;
An' I kissed my gal an' boy,
An' was half afaint with joy.

Then I wrote that night to Dad,
"Don't you worry 'bout the lad,
'Cause he wrote in his school-han'
Words that we could understan'."

AS WELL AS I.

The Daughter of the House Soliloquizes.

No, my mother does not look as well as I,
For the days of her appearing well, are by:
She can sew a bit, and sweep a bit, and fry—
    But she doesn't look well
    When I entertain a swell,
In the parlor, and she happens to be nigh.
    She is good to meet alone
    When the brilliant ones are flown;
    When the world seems all in vain,
    She can soothe away the pain;
She can kiss away the tear-drops if I cry;
    But reluctantly I state
    She is not quite up-to-date,
And is apt to set the functions all awry.

No, my mother cannot talk as well as I,
And we often wish she wouldn't even try.
She can give the smartest joker his reply,
    But her nouns and verbs, you see,
    Do not always quite agree;
And my guests are prone to laugh upon the sly.
    When we sit and talk alone,
    With her arms around me thrown,
    And my head upon her breast
    In delicious home-made rest,
No raconteur can a moment with her vie;
    But she does not always know
    When her words should stop or flow;
And her stories of the past are rather dry.

No, my mother cannot sing as well as I:
She is apt to pitch it low or hold it high;
And her methods all my master's rules defy.
    But the time seems very near
    When she carolled "Hush, my dear",
As in fancy 'mid the cradle-depths I lie.
    And I fell asleep ere long,
    Dreaming angels sang the song;
    And the loveliest one was she,
    Of the hosts that guarded me;
And she often talks about it, with a sigh.
    But those baby-days are fled:
    There are other songs ahead,
And I have to catch the chances as they fly.

No, my mother is not near so strong as I:
She is nervous; and I often can espy
That her tears have not sufficient time to dry.
    She has griefs I do not know,
    As the years relentless flow,
And as one by one her visions fade and die.
    There is sadness in her heart,
    That she keeps from me apart;
    There are sorrows, many a while,
    That she smothers with a smile;
When she weeps, I cannot always ask her why.
    And I fear—or guess—or know—
    I myself will have to go
Through the same forlorn experience—by-and-by!

"—THEY'S SOMETHIN' HERE THAT'S WRONG"

FIXING THE CLOCK.

It's jest as fawther said it was—they's somethin' here that's wrong;
The gran'ther-clock is ailin' sir—we're glad you come along.
It stood an' sulked a week or two, an' wouldn't tick or ring,
Or run its han's aroun' its face, or do a blessed thing.

It's old enough to hev a rest, as people say, you know;
We often think it started out a thousan' year ago.
An' Cousin Pete, who sets an' tells us stories in the dark,
He wonders ef it give the time for Noarh in the ark.

We're glad it's goin' to start ag'in; for when it ain't no good,
It makes a sort o' friendly fuss all through the neighborhood;
The folks inquire as if 'twas folks, an' stop us on the way,
An' anxiously they ask us how the ol' clock is today.

They's lots o' time-machines aroun' that have a deal o' lack,
An' need a steady gran'ther-clock to keep 'em on the track;
I've seen folks stan' out in the road, an' wait an' listen like,
To set their watch by this 'ere clock, as soon's they heard it strike.

We're glad it stopped, though; so's that you could take it all apart,
An' we could see its thinkin' works, an' where it kep' its heart;
An' why, before it's goin' to strike, four minutes an' a half,
It sort o' up an' chuckles, like, as ef it meant to laugh;

An' how it keeps the memory good, although it's got so old,
An' how it knows the moon is new, or full o' yeller gold;
An' tells it with its picture-moons, so's we can know it nigh
As well as ef we went out-door an' found it in the sky;

An' ef it ever has the blues, alone there night an' day,
An' how it come to know the facts, when baby went away;
For half the night there through the dark a-cryin' in our bed,
We heard it talkin' to itself—"She's dead—she's dead—she's dead!"

An' then I guess I went to sleep, an' dreamed a little while,
An' thought I saw her in the clouds, an' knew her by her smile;
An' when the sunrise woke me up—'twas maybe six or seven—
It changed its mind, an' says to me, "In Heaven—in Heaven—in
Heaven!"

THE MOCKING-BIRD.

A True Story.

Of manner shy, of gleaming eye,
  And dainty bill and feather,
With kindly word, a mocking-bird
  Was sent from balmy weather;
From oaks and pines, and em'rald vines,
  And flow'rets gently clinging;
From grassy leas of orange-trees,
  And comrades near him singing.

The chill and rime of Northern clime
  Hung round him like a tether;
He beat and pressed his wiry nest,
  And yearned for happy weather.
The weeks were long, he gave no song,
  However wiled or bidden;
Each jewelled note within his throat
  Was but a treasure hidden.

Of orange-blooms and rare perfumes
  And buds and leaves together,
With kind intent, a box was sent
  From out the South-land weather:

'Gainst looks of rage, into the cage
  A gentle finger pressed them:
By rapture stirred, the mocking-bird
  With cries of joy caressed them!

Then came his song, as sweet and strong
  As on his native heather:
He trilled with ease the psalms and glees
  That grace the loveliest weather.
None may indite what message bright
  Those perfumed leaves were bringing:
We only say, that since that day,
  Our exile-bird is singing!

UP IN THE LOFT.

Up in the loft, 'mid scented clover,
Five of us perched and talked it over;
Talked of the years that lagged and waited,
Full of the gold of Fancy freighted;
Full of the joys that Hope was living—
Joys that the world is slow in giving;
Full of the honors Youth can spread
    Over its own fair head.
Tom was a colonel brave and comely,
There in his worsted garments homely;
Jack was a doctor all were seeking,
Jem was a lawyer, glib of speaking;
Fred as a merchant bought and sold
Half of the world for leaves of gold;
And I was sailing the wide seas over,
There in my ship of scented clover.

Up in the tomb of the blossoms sitting,
Ghosts of the past were round us flitting;
Forms that magical deeds had done,
    Came to us one by one;
All of the tales we had heard and read,
    Now were sung or said.
Tom of the knights with helmets glancing,
Under their snow-white plumage dancing;
Jem of the genii weird of mission—
Jack of the sages' cold ambition:
Fred of the lamp which, dim and old
Lighted Aladdin to fame and gold;

And I was at heart a Sindbad rover,
Gathering gems in a vale of clover.

Up in the couch of the grasses lying,
There as the winds outside were sighing,
There in that field of fragrant clover,
Under the barn-roof's trusted cover,
All of us whispered some sweetheart-name—
    Haply no two the same;
All of us murmured secrets there,
    Of tiny maidens fair:
In that chapel of scented clover,
Each of us vowed himself a lover.
How did the castles we were building
Fall with the sunrise' fragile gilding!
How were the hopes Desire was giving
Crushed in the wear and tear of living!
How, in the noontide's steady glare,
    Gone are our maidens fair!
Tom's, in a few short years, sedately
Married a judge, severe and stately:
Jack had the "mitten" prematurely,
Jem has a wife he loves unsurely;
Fred has one who, dainty elf,
Married his money, and not himself;
And she whose image thoughtfully gay
Lit brightest the loft on that winter day,
Sleeps, when the summer winds fly over,
Solemnly 'neath the blossomed clover.

TO A DEAD BIRD.

Poor, perished thing,
How helpless, now, thy angel-painted wing;
How tired of death the unaffected grace
That lingers on thy little feathered face!
Could any gem that mortals choose to prize
Assume to match the radiance of thine eyes?
Some man destroyed what ne'er again can be,
In killing thee.

Say, silent thing:
Hadst thou the Heaven-invented gift to sing?
Couldst chant a sonnet, undefiled by art,
And thrill and win the chosen of thy heart?
Couldst hush the silent sobbing of the air,
With strains of jewelled laughter, free from care?
One fancies some of God's unsullied glee
Went back with thee.

Didst love to fling
Thyself upon the swelling breast of Spring?
Didst joy to thread the airy lanes with ease,
Or find a swaying throne among the trees?
With dainty prow and firmly planted sail,
Couldst ride along the billows of the gale?
Heaven meant the earth and azure safe and free,
For such as thee.

But, plumaged thing,
If deathly splendor can a comfort bring,
If but thy body, from its sweet control,
May send a message to the restless soul,
Rejoice: it hath a more than royal bed:
Thy mausoleum is my lady's head.
And I can fancy many swains I see,
That envy thee!

THE TWO BOYS.

The "Tot" Discourses.

Of all the peoples in this town,
  So far as I can see,
The best two fellows, up and down,
  Is Uncle Joe an' me.
We found each other long ago—
How much it is I can't quite know—
I guess a thousan' years or so—
  An' never didn't agree.

We know where all the bluejays nest,
  Does Uncle Joe an' me,
An' when the robins sings the best,
  An' where the squirrels be;
An' when the rabbits romp an' play,
An' where the biggest woodchucks stay,
An' where the owl sleeps every day,
  An' where the thrushes be.

When we drive out he lets me drive,
  An' then we both agree
There ain't two bigger sports alive,
  Than Uncle Joe an' me.
He says he'd just as lives as not
Lend me the fastest horse he's got,
He wouldn't let no other "tot"
  Take hold the reins, you see!

We know the biggest stories, too,
  Does Uncle Joe an' me,

An' some of 'em is partly true,
  An' some is goin' to be;
'Bout Injuns, full of scalps an' noise,
An' giants that had trees fur toys,
An' how things was when we was boys—
  Some years ago, you see!

My mommer says we've got to die,
  An' angels live an' be,
An' go an' dwell up in the sky,
  From sin forever free;
But that's what I don't mean to do,
Till Uncle Joe gets started, too:
For Heaven would be most awful blue,
  'Thout Uncle Joe an' me!

BLOWING THE FEATHER.

Blowing the feather, ten together
   Sat in the lamplight's honest glare;
While outside, the lips of the weather
   Hurried the leaflets here and there.
Blowing the feather, ten together
   Laughed in the lamplight's cozy glare.

At right of the feather, two together
   Merrily sat—a rival pair:
Each of the swains was wondering whether
   That sweet maiden over there—
   She with the skeins of golden hair
Holding those two with Love's strong tether—
   Had for either a tender care.

Left of the feather, two together
   Laughingly sat—another pair;
   One was a man of quiet air,
   And one was this maid with the golden hair.
He might have been—but was not—her brother;
They never deigned to glance at each other—
   Or had for a neighbor a word to spare;
Watching, with laughs they tried to smother,
   The two fierce rivals over there.

"Now," said the maid, "who gets the feather,
   Over his heart this rose may wear!"
   Then there was grasping here and there—
Then there were breaths that rushed together;
   All were striving, except the pair
   Sitting so calmly, chair by chair,

Silently watching the dancing feather:
  The man with the cool and dreamy air,
  And the laughing maid with golden hair.

Front of the rivals stopped the feather;
  One was grasping, with eager air,
And one was flushed as the frosted heather,
  Blowing the white-winged omen where
  His rival should miss it, in despair;
But straight it flew, o'er the surface wide,
To the man who sat at the farther side—
  He of the quiet and dreamy air:
"All things come, if we do but wait",
He said to the maiden, calm as Fate,
  And offered his heart to the fingers fair.
The maiden turned as white as the feather,
  Then red as the rose, as she pinned it there.

HARVESTS.

Harvests of old, through gold-mines of the peasant,
Delved thy forged sickle—a silvery crescent;
In the cool breeze or the thick sultry weather,
Toiled the strong lad and the maiden together.
Winsomeness into the Eden-curse bringing,
Oft did they charm sober toil with their singing;
Then when the harvest-moon rose in its splendor,
Homeward they fared, oft with words that were tender,
Or through the silver-strown song's gallant measures,
Rumbled the wains with their rish golden treasures.

Harvests less old!—still the memory lingers
Of thy broad blade with its tapering fingers;
How as it swung came the tremulous sighing
Of the trim grain-plants so suddenly dying!
How, a rude music that baffles forgetting
Rang out the song of the scythe in its whetting;
How the glum toiler or jest-loving fellow
Lunched in a shade of their wide camps of yellow,
Gossiping e'en as the idlest of woman—
Showing that both of the sexes are human!

Harvests today! through the grain-forest sweeping
Comes like a cyclone an engine of reaping.
Reaper, and gleaner, and old-fashioned peasant
Flee from this monster—grim child of the present;
Sickle and scythe, and the flail for the threshing
Fused into wheels, through the meadows go crashing.
All of the harvest-songs vanish before us,
Blended and lost in this grand metal chorus.
Such are the harvests these rushing days fling us:
What will the twentieth century bring us?

STARS OF THE GRASSES.

Fireflies! fireflies! fragments of light,
Leading through darkness the careless sight—
Tremulous stars of the lower night;

Living lamps in the green below,
Clinging and swinging to and fro,
Where the forests of grasses grow;

How can we say but yonder star,
Glittering in the blue afar,
May be conscious, as insects are?

Greater and stronger, but still as you,
Oft it will vanish from our view,
Then will glitter, as fired anew.

E'en as an insect, bye and bye
Yonder star in its turn must die,
Making a death-bed of the sky.

GOOD-BYE, OLD HORSE.

The pleasant days have gone their ways, the world is getting old,
The wind is in the north again—the air is damp and cold;
They turn their heads and laugh at us—those days we used to win—
And Fortune when we ask for her, sends word she isn't in.
The earth is growing bare and bleak, and clouds are in the sky;
So I must go and find the sun: my dear old horse, good-bye!

You had a speed and I a rein we both knew how to trust:
Oh 'twas a mighty lively rig that gave us any dust!
We made a race-track of the road whene'er we had a mind,
And you had not the faculty of following on behind.
But luck went off another way, and never told us why:—
And so I've got to walk a bit:—my dear old horse, good-bye!

One night we met a robber band with whom we couldn't agree—
And one caressed you by the bit, and one took charge of me.
I knocked mine over with the whip, and yours you trampled down,
And showed the rest a set of heels unrivalled in the town.
I said, "Old man, we'll never part till one of us shall die":
But Ruin sneers at hearts and hands—good-bye, old friend, good-bye!

One merry eve when ruby wine had turned my brain to lead,
Beside the road when half-way home I stopped and went to bed.
But I was watched by chivalry all through my night's disgrace:
For when I woke, your warm sweet nose was cuddling round my face.
You vowed no harm should come to me, with you a-lingering nigh:
I'd stay by you now if I could—good-bye, old horse, good-bye!

I think and hope I'm leaving you in good and friendly hands—
I feel as if you'd think of me in distant seas and lands;
And if my fate turns round again, and Effort serves me true,
There'll come first thing across the space, a telegram for you.
I hope that yet some happy days we'll capture, you and I,
And golden stables shall be yours, in Heaven, bye and bye!

Songs of the Rivers.

TO GO A-SWIMMING.

There's a red-letter page that is brighter for its age,
  And the finger-marks of Time are never dimming;
It has very much to say of a hot summer day,
  When we fellows ran away, to go a-swimming.
Creeping through lengthy grass while dancing shadows pass,
Threading deep haunted woods where the squirrel stows his goods,
And birds nested high teach their little ones to fly,
Where the grape-cluster shines in a wilderness of vines,
Where are mossy pillows green not a slumberer hath seen,
And the red flowers grow in a blossom-drift of snow;—
It was maybe twice as gay that we felt a bit astray,
  When we fellows ran away, to go a-swimming!

And the river and the pool were so heaven-like and cool,
  With fresh baby-breezes over-skimming;
Everything well contrived for a pleasure short-lived,
  When we runaways arrived to go a-swimming!
Now all ready—now a plunge! and our bodies, like a sponge
That unduly dry has been, seem to drink the water in;
We are groping in the caves of the cold silent waves,
We are climbing to the air, flinging torrents from our hair,
And we struggle to and fro through the ripples' gentle flow,
And we duels gaily fight with the plashing waters bright,
On each other, through the fray, flinging barrels-full of spray;
  Oh! the mad and merry day we went a-swimming!

Now the moral of this rhyme is for youth's careless time,
  Full of good, sober counsel it is brimming:
In your labor or your play, your superiors obey;
  Don't you ever run away to go a-swimming.

Though the flower-jewels shine with a radiance divine,
And the daisy-blossoms creep in the meadows half asleep,
And the clouds are like a high floating castle in the sky,
And the forest-branches dumb wink and beckon you to come,
And a shady nook you know where the dainty billows flow,
Whose delicious quiet charms would fold you in their arms—
Be obedient while you may; on the shore of duty stay;
Don't you ever run away to go a-swimming!

"WHERE WE WATERED THE TEAM"

WHERE WE WATERED THE TEAM.

The sky was a blaze; but the forest's green haze
Made our journey a dream;
And torn shadows fell like the fringe of a spell—
Where we watered the team.
The flower-bushes stood—radiant belles of the wood—
In their jewels around;
A grass-forest grew and incumbered our view
Of the hills of the ground.

Sweet rivulets pressed from a mountain's high crest,
Like arrows agleam;
Flowed in beauty and mirth the white blood of the earth,
Where we watered the team.
It daintily flung, silent shadows among,
Bright jewels of sound;
Thus crooning a free merry song of the sea—
Whence it came—where 'twas bound.

There was music to spare in the leaf-scented air,
Where we watered the team;
Chanted robin and thrush, in the half-sacred hush,
Their melodious theme.
And the clear water sung, to the heart as it clung
Of a tree that was prone;
And the horses' soft lips in sweet tremulous sips
Had a chant of their own.

Mid the rest-giving din, a bright chalice of tin
Threw its welcoming beam;
And we drank to the health of this fragment of wealth,
When we'd watered the team.
We were wondering much, as the wave's cooling touch
Through our beings was strown,
If it were not a taste of the stream that John traced
To the depths of the throne.

CHANT OF THE ST. LAWRENCE.

I am marching to the sea—
To my king, the mighty sea;
In his tent he waits for me—
In his tent, with walls of blue,
Decked with flags of brightest hue,
In his starlit, sunlit tent,
O'er the head in splendor bent.

I have messages in store,
For my king, the mighty sea:
Great Superior's solemn word,
Huron's answering voice is heard.
Erie's shelving walls of land,
Clad with wealth and comfort o'er;
Stern Niagara's thunder-pour,
Great Ontario's prosperous strand
Decked with city-pictures grand—
All send messages by me,
To their king, the mighty sea.

All my treasures I must leave—
All my thousand tree-fringed isles,
All my shore-hills clad in smiles—
All the shadows that they weave,
All my woods, with eyes of blue,
All the cottages of white,

Bathed in dim reflected light;
  Would that I might take them too,
Floating eastward down with me,
For an offering to the sea!

Stately ships with plumes of black,
Follow on my gleaming track;
Villages with sails of white,
Decked with banners brave and bright;
Funeral-trains of forest-trees,
Journey with me to the seas—
Travel with me toward the main—
March amid my glittering train.

Down the rapid's giddy stair
  Rush I headlong as in fear;
Past the crags that linger there—
  Past th' old gray rock's constant sneer,
To my death-like, deathless fate,
Where my lord and king doth wait.
Panic-struck, I rush and rave,
As some mortals toward the grave,
Rush and rave and hurry on,
With my task no nearer won.
But or tranquil or in haste,
Frowning wild or placid-faced,
Eastward still my soul is set:
I am loyal, even yet!

Times, in broad blue lakes I tarry,
  Kept in couches soft and low;
Lulled to sleep as if by fairy,
  Breeze-caresses sweep my brow.
Sun-caresses thrill my soul,
Shadow-hands my ways control;
In the night's unlaughing glee,
Stars come out and smile at me;
Zephyrs from the wooded west,
Pause awhile, with me to rest.
"Here", I plead, "that I might stay
Many a night and many a day!"

But the cry is "Onward! On!"
Never, till my journey's done,
Can I tarry well or long,
Can I hush my marching-song.
I am marching to the sea—
To my king, the mighty sea;
In his tent he waits for me,
In his tent, with walls of blue,
Decked with flags of brightest hue
In his starlit, sunlit tent,
O'er the head in splendor bent;
On his calm, majestic breast,
I will lie, in changeful rest.

THE OARSMAN'S STORY.

Hold it steady—don't disturb him—give him leeway for to bite—
Yes, you've got him! reel him careful, for he'll make a lovely fight!
O my gracious! now you've lost him, an' he's swiped your hook an' bait!
Never mind; we'll throw another; he will stan' around an' wait.
It's a reason for our thinkin' that the fish are slow to feel,
That their appetites 'll sharpen, when they get a taste o' steel!

Now, that sort o' half reminds me of a bass I used to know,
That was brains from prow to rudder, if a fish was ever so;
For he stole my bait off handy every time I throwed it in,
An' then flopped up from the water with a cunnin' sort o' grin;
An' I fin'lly named him Lawyer; for he'd leave the hook as bare
As a client in a court-room with atturneys fur to spare.

An' I worked him late an' early, an' I give him all the chance
That a fish was ever offered, for to take a river-dance;
But he made the same division an' he drawed it very fine,
Taking fur himself the minny—leavin' me the hook an' line;
An' I struggled late and early with my fish-poles an' my reels,
An' my time an' strength an' minnies—jest to give that fish his meals.

An' it fin'lly come to askin' whether natives on the shore,
That had paddled through the river for a forty year or more,
Should be beaten every summer by a feller, it appears,
Who had only swum the water for a half a dozen years;
An' two nights I laid a-thinkin' how to work it on him slick,
An' to play the little lawyer one good everlastin' trick.

Then I built a queer contraption strung with new-invented crooks—
'Twas a circus made of minnies an' a side-show full o' hooks;
An' I don't suppose a critter could go near it head or tail,
But 'twas sure to catch him somehow, an' to hold him like a nail;

An' I loudly hollered "Glory!" an' was full o' joy an' pride,
When that afternoon I snapped him, with a fish-hook in his side!

But he mildly gazed upon me, as I drawed him up an' near,
With a look of disappointment in his eye so black an' clear;
An' he seemed to say as reg'lar as a fish with words to spare,
"Now, you know to make it decent you are bound to catch me fair!
You an' I has been a-strivin' at a scientific game,
An' to treat me foul an' sneaky is an everlastin' shame!"

Then I ans'rs, "Do you mean it—do you think it—straight an' true?"
An' he winked his eye like sayin', "Yes, by gracious, sir, I do!"
An' I picked the fish-hook from him, usin' most unusual care,
An' he seemed to whisper, "Thank you; but it's only just an' fair!"
An' I cut off my new fish-hooks—all the whole infernal set—
An' I throwed 'em in the river, and they're in the river yet.

An' I launched my friend a-floatin' in the water cold an' blue,
An' he flopped a sort of "Thank you", as he disappeared from view;
An' he never stole a minny nor seemed ready to commence,
Though he's sort o' hung around me in the water ever sence;
An' I often think the feller means to pay me back ag'in,
An' now acts as my atturney fur to rope the others in;

But he started me a-thinkin': When you fish, as fish you will,
Be a sport an' not a butcher; try to catch an' not to kill;
Keep enough to serve your eatin', let the surplus fellers go;
Send the small ones to their mothers—give 'em time to fat an grow.
An' when pullin' in the fishes, don't be slow to recollect
To secure 'em in a manner not to forfeit their respect.

OUT OF ALEXANDR' BAY.

A January Fish-Story.

Poke the fire a little, children, till the log begins to blaze,
For the January blizzards hev a lot of frosty ways;
Bring the apples an' the doughnuts, an'—the cider, understan',
An' be mighty sure to place 'em some'at handy to the han';
An' I'll string you up a story illustrative of the way
That I used to go a-fishing out of Alexandr' Bay.

First, I asked the wind an' current fur to furnish me a lift,
Then I sailed away a distance in my double-p'inted skift;
An' I tuk it when desirous of a half a day alone,
Fur the biggest of the fishes doesn't like a human tone.
An' I recollect I anchored on one mornin' bright an' clear,
Where the basses used to gather in that season of the year.

When I found 'em, they was huddled near a little islan'-beach,
An' they measured—O my gracious, twice as much as I ken reach
(An' I don't believe there's any hev their arms in a posish
Fur to stretch 'em more than I ken, in describin' of a fish);
An' the mornin' was so gentle, an' the water was so clear,
I cud see 'em smell my minny jus' as if they all was here.

But a lot o' rich New Yorkers hed their summer houses nigh,
An' my gracious them 'er fishes was a-eatin' cake an' pie!
Cooks hed throwed it in the river when it cluttered up a dish,
An' I s'pose it tasted better to the fishes, than a fish;
An' I whispered to my conscience, "You are very near a fool,
Ef you waste your time a-danglin' overneath a boardin'-school!"

Then my conscience answered, "Stiddy; keep a-givin 'em the bait!
There is al'ays blessin's comin' to a feller that can wait."

An' I kep' a peekin' down'ard so 's to see how matters stood,
An' I held a lively minny jus' as near 'em as I could;
An' I meant it as a primium fer the scholars; but alas!
Not a single one would offer fur to jine my cookin'-class!

Then they sort o' laid an' rested in the water still an' deep,
An' they dropped their noses down'ard, an' appeared to go to sleep;
An' they nestled near and nearer to the river's sandy floor,
An' I listened till I reckoned I could hear the fellers snore!
An' I says, "Lie still and slumber; I'm a-watching o'er your bed;
If you'll only wake up hungry, here is blessin's on your head!

Bye an' bye the leader started, scratched his for'ead with a fin,
An' he stretched an' yawned a little, an' my bait it wiggled in
('Twas a knowin' breed o' minnies we was rearin' at the Bay),
An' the bass he shut his mouth up, an' the hook got in the way;
An' before he hed the priv'lege fur to flop a single note,
He had left his loved companions, an' had started for the boat.

Then I winked unto the minny, an' I thought I see him grin,
An' I 'magine he enjoyed it, so I sent him down ag'in;
An' he run among 'em lively—like a wiggler in a cup;
An' kep' knockin' at their doorways, till he woke another up;
An' the fish embraced his caller, more in passion than in love;
An' immediately started for the happy land above.

One by one the others wakened, an' the word was passed aroun'
There was somethin' there fur nothin' that hed jus' come into town;
An' they soon was crazy fur it—an' the smartest of 'em led
(Fur a fish is partly human, as I think I al'ays said):
An' may Ananias' spirit come and visit me tonight,
Ef them everlastin' fishes didn't stan' in line to bite!

An' my boat was overloaded till it sort o' sagged an' stuck,
An' I sold 'em out in messes to some fellers scant of luck;
An' some fifty reputations as a fisherman, no doubt,
Was established on the fishes I'm a-tellin' ye about;
Anyhow, the rich New Yorkers, they was buyin' all the way
From the islan' of the basses into Alexandr' Bay.

FROM CORN-FIELD TO RIVER.

Yes, a seashore swimmin'-hole in a manner is excitin'—
Jumpin' billows like a hoop—or with ram-like waves a-fightin',
Beddin' in the flea-bit sand tryin' to improve the weather—
In a pair of overhauls an' a shirt-waist sewed together;
But for me I must agree that the ocean ain't a trimmin'
To the day we ran away from the fields, to go a-swimmin'!
[Thus said Ahab Adams, riding in "my auto-mo-what-is-it?"
To his brother Daniel Adams from Montana on a visit.]

What an afternoon that was!—all creation seemed a-burnin'!
Sim an' Jim an' me an' you agricult'ral tricks was learnin';
'Mongst the corn an' punkin vines for the world's advancement growin',
We four boys was takin' walks where the baked world needed hoein'.

What a hot-house day it was! sun a bonfire just above us;
Air as still as grassy graves of the folks that used to love us;
Skies as clear as babies' eyes—old moon grinned at our condition;
Cloud or cloudlet anywhere was an unknown proposition.
So we done the horses' work, while they stood 'neath shade-trees charmin'
(Cultivators wan't yet made, so that men could ride their farmin').

An' we walked an' hoed an' arg'ed various matters of creation
That would make us think way off, an' forget our perspiration:
Wondered 'bout the steamboat craft ploughin' up a watery furrow,
Deacon Smith had seen one day when he went to Middleborough;
Wondered at the railroad trains—how there ever come to be one—
If they'd some time skip our way—or we'd ever git to see one;
Talked about the stars on high—mostly suns of long existence—
Glad, if they was like *our* sun, they knowed how to keep their distance;
Talked about the 'lectric wire that the city-folks was gettin'—
Wondered how they kep' the news, when 'twas rainy, from a wettin';

Talked about the winter school; how we worked there like the dickens,
On the sums; an' how, somehow, ans'ers wan't as flush as lickin's;
How warm Sundays growed the sermons; how we never got to miss one;
Wondered if the other world had a corn-field hot as this one;
Talked our high ambitions higher, mourned the poverty that bound us—
Talked of all the pretty gals for ten mile or so around us;
Hoein' with our minds an' hearts facts we'd noticed or been taught of:
Several things that Markham's fool mebby never even thought of.

But while we was bakin' there, raisin' fodder for the cattle,
In the road some rods away we could hear a wagon rattle;
It was Dad, a-drivin' off to'ds the village, with the women;
An' I recollect you said, "Boys, le's sneak an' go a-swimmin'!"

I hev since been up an' down through agreements an' contentions;
I hev even helped to run legislaters an' conventions;
But for unanimity right up equal to my notion,
I hev never seen it yet, since the time you made that motion.

How we crept off through the woods till we found that blessed river!
How we dove into its depths, with a first delicious shiver!
How we paddled up an' down! How we splashed each others' faces!
How we tunnelled through the water, comin' up in different places!
How we towed each other round by the hair an' heels alternit!
How a half of us could swim an' the others tried to learn it!
How we envied everything that was ever scaled or finny!
"This", I recollect you said, "beats the corn-field all to Guinea!"

Yes, 'twas heaven! an' when 'twas through nothin' made it less elatin',
'Ceptin' Dad upon the bank, with some birch-sticks, calmly waitin'.

Songs of the Mountains.

PROLOGUE.

The mountains! the mountains!
With crag-step rough and steep;
With silent form and hooded storm,
And avalanche asleep;
Whose tops are hieroglyphics
By fire and tempest wrought,
That human race can never trace
Till God the key has brought.

The mountains! the mountains!
When fall the drenching rains,
That glide and creep, that rush and leap
To find their ocean-plains!
When Winter with loud trumpet
But soft and silent tramp,
Chains brook and rill, and makes each hill
A white tent of his camp!

The mountains! the mountains!
With gardens in their keep:
With bloom that shines, and emerald vines,
And arbors still and deep!
E'en in the tropic's empire,
Like floral worlds they tower;
For every zone that earth has known,
Will send a greeting-flower.

The mountains! the mountains!
Where forests live and die;
Where through long years tree-mountaineers
Are struggling toward the sky,

With combats fierce though silent,
  With struggles brave and long;
While in their tops the wind oft stops
  To sing their battle-song.

The mountains! the mountains!
  That harbor beasts of prey;
Where wild-dogs howl and panthers prowl
  And reptiles shun the day;
Where serpents creep and clamber,
  Where eagle-broods are fed;
And caved from air the sullen bear
  Has found his winter bed.

The mountains! the mountains!
  Where sickness, pain, and care
'Gainst ramparts high may rest their eye,
  And drink the creamy air;
Where smile the clustered landscapes,
  Where robins brood and nest;
And Nature's child with song beguiled
  May on her bosom rest.

The mountains! the mountains!
  Great watch-tower tops have they,
Whence, starred and clear, Heaven seems so near,
  And earth so far away!
Whence one may call to Jesus,
  Who mused on hills alone,
Or hearts devote to Him who wrote
  The mountain-page of stone.

" WHERE SMILE THE CLUSTERED LANDSCAPES "

TO THE MOUNTAIN PROFILE.

From Clara's Mind.

Giant of old, formed in the mould
Of some god of the past,
What wouldst thou say if thy lips of gray
Could speak at last?

Couldst thou not tell all that befell
At the mountain's fierce birth,
When fiends of fire made a red pyre
Of the desolate earth?

Wast thou not here when from the drear
Snowy hills of the North,
Glaciers of gray from their country astray
Sailed in majesty forth?

Was it a crime in some dead time,
That imprisoned thee there?
Penitent now, is that sad brow
Lifted in prayer?

When the black storm winds its cold form
About thy face,
Dost thou not fear destruction near,
Last of thy race?

Or, when the sun, life-giving one,
Cheers the world and the sky,
Dost thou e'er groan lest while Earth holds her own,
Thou canst not die?

TO THE SAME.

From Clara's Big Brother's Mind.

Weary old face on the precipice glowering,
What is there in you so vastly o'erpowering?
Why, as men gaze, is their fancy a slave of you—
Why do the women so frequently rave of you?
Why with the lens do they render absurder you—
Why upon plaques do they maltreat and murder you?
Though you've no visible means of restraining it,
Still, you might venture some mode of explaining it!

Many a novelist eagerly wrote of you—
Poets have made much prosodical note of you—
Orators oft have had somewhat to say of you—
Artists have offered no end of display of you;
How do you do it?—while, fatly or meagerly,
Real men are striving for notice so eagerly?
Savage old face on the precipice slumbering,
When the night hours their black minutes are numbering,
Say! are the sprites with sweet visions e'er storing you,
Made up of ladies perversely adoring you?
How would you look, if effusively facing them?
How would they act if you spoke of embracing them?
How would your cold kisses prove indigestible,
Nature's own Frankenstein, crude and detestable!

You must have met with some startling calamities:
You have no body, no arms, no extremities.
Or they are, if we persist in presuming them,
Buried in rock, with no hope of exhuming them.

Even your face—one may see, with facility,
Stands off in parts that prevent sociability
(Unlike those maidens who nourish the pride of you);
When one goes round to a different side of you,
Then you appear, to the veriest slow body,
Merely a wink and a blink and a nobody!

Still keep your head 'mid the mountains' rough
    comeliness—
Answer no questions, grim fragment of homeliness:
Many a boor, from mere lack of loquacity,
Builds up a good name for mental capacity:
Many a fool is a wise man instead to us,
Just from the things that he never has said to us.

Long as the roads are their passengers numbering,
Long as the stage through the forest is lumbering,
Long as the summer-girl washes her freckles in,
Long as the inn-keeper gathers his shekels in,
Long as good folk in vacuity sorrowing
Are from the past exclamation-points borrowing,
Stay where you are, neatly shelved curiosity—
Known as the mountain's most monstrous mon-
    strosity!

IN THE MOUNTAINS, YOU KNOW.

Yes, old fellow, I went to the mountains, you know,
Where the hyacinths bloom and the daffodils blow;
For my sister was there with her bevy of seven;
They are all of them angels, but still out of heaven.
'Twas "Oh, Uncle, you've come!" and with love-seasoned pats,
Like a frolicsome parcel of juvenile cats,
They hung to me, clung to me, wouldn't let me go,
On the first day I got to the mountains, you know.

Then a walk through the meadows suggested to me
An escape from the noise, and a think, don't you see;
So I roamed in the sweet-smelling grasses afar,
And I borrowed a match and I lit a cigar;
Then I saw through the fence, lying prone and asleep,
A peculiar mild-countenanced horn-handled sheep;
So I climbed to his side and I kindly bent low,
And awoke him to see what he'd do, don't you know.

And I saw, very soon; for he rose to his feet,
And commenced a peculiar and guarded retreat;
Retreated—ah—backward—face toward me, I mean,
Just the same as folks do from a king or a queen;
And I pitied him much for the fear he displayed,
And I said, "My dear chappie, now don't be afraid!"
And I judge he was not: for, dispenser of woe,
He came at me as if from a gun, don't you know!

And I skipped like a deer, or a yacht in a breeze,
In a way that distended my pants at the knees;
And, to uttermost speed by the animal pressed,
I relinquished my coat and my necktie and vest;

And I went round the field, trying hard for first
place,
Like a sprinter that's trying to capture a race;
And, "We'll bet on you, Uncle!" was screeched to
and fro;
For the children had climbed on the fence, don't
you know.

As was afterwards said, 'twas quite touching to see
That undignified creature's attachment for me;
And wherever my footsteps would go, don't you mind,
The diminutive monster was not far behind!
And he seemed to have picked up a notion, indeed,
That his mission on earth was to further my speed;
And I think that we furnished a capital show
To the people that happened to pass, don't you know!

Then a handsome young lady stepped over the stile,
With a blessed tin dipper of salt, and a smile;
And she said, "Come, Dick, dear!" (that's the name
that *I* keep,
But I'm glad that 'twas also the name of the sheep;
For he went to the maid to be fed and caressed,
While I walked down the road for a while and re-
dressed);
And I've made up my mind that if *she'll* see it so,
I will marry that girl in the fall, don't you know!

SOME COUNTRY SOLACE.

Late Evening.

From the city's constant clatter,
  I have come, with purpose deep
Not to healthy grow, or fatter,
  But to sleep, and sleep, and sleep.
Not so much in hours of night-time
  (City habits capture them!)
For I rather think the right time
  Is from two to eight A. M.
Oh the comfort and completeness
  Of these balmy morning naps!
'Tis because they hold the sweetness
  Found in stolen goods, perhaps.
(Steal the golden locks one may,
From the foretop of the day.)

Scarce could words contrive the shaping
Of the noise that I'm escaping!—
Town utilities and follies:
Steam-cars, horse-cars, air-cars, trollies,
Butcher-boys, the distance spurning,
  Strewing flesh the city o'er;
Bottle-milkmen, fiercely churning
  Their white wares from door to door;
Cats through garden-jungles prowling,
Dogs with death-notes in their howling,
All the highways' crash and clatter—
All the byways' clash and chatter;
Postman's whistle, iceman's yelling,
Huckster's plea for double-selling;
Door-bells, school-bells, fire-bells—every

Kind of bell's acoustic slavery:
All these helped me toward obeying
Solomon's most lively saying,
While I wondered at his prizing
Of the old ant's early rising,
So as in soft words to coddle
Her, and pose her as a model!

Early Morning.

How we miss the bliss we aim for!
Surely 'tis not this I came for:
Hear the rooster's trumpet, shaming
  All who do not greet the morn!
Hear the hen's wild song, proclaiming
  That another hope is born!
Hear the wakeful cattle lowing
  For the gardens of the herds;
Hear on air the maids bestowing
  Lexicons of damaged words;
Hear the robins' notes inspiring
  You to drink those rills of sound;
Hear the sparrows, loud inquiring
  Where the early worm is found!
Then back to your covert creeping,
Try again the art of sleeping,
  With such critics grouped around.

I can stand the fitful walker,
  Oft he comes—but oft he goes;
But that everlasting talker
  Underneath the window's nose!
Words, and words, without endeavor,
Speech-brook, flowing on forever!
Talking every subject weary,
Till it wilts—a phantom dreary;
Pauseless he—this rural Solon;
Comma, period, semicolon,
None of these will he set free.

Oh what blessedness, if he
  Would cut loose those pauses' tether,
And like old Lord Timothy,
  Let them all appear together!

From the country's clash and chatter,
  Creep I, not by half so merry,
And, to try and mend the matter,
  Seek the silent cemetery.
There, where sleeping is the fashion,
  I, by some lone grave, mayhap,
Can indulge my silent passion,
  And secure a morning nap.
Even then, some early-rising
  Bug may see me, I suppose,
And begin the day by sizing
  The compartments of my nose.
Only dead folks, buried deep,
They can sleep, and sleep, and sleep.

THE MAID OF THE MOUNTAIN.

It was morning 'mongst the hill-tops, with a golden day begun,
And the Old Man of the Mountain caught the radiance of the sun,
And some fleecy clouds were hanging o'er his brow serene and high,
And the faded moon was drifting in the ocean of the sky;
While the banks along the lakelet were with breezes hovered o'er,
And the ripples whispered softly to the pebbles on the shore.

Now a summer-girl had wandered on her nimble steed of steel,
And was gazing on the water, with a white hand on her wheel.
Then her handsome eyes uplifted, as an eagle sought his nest,
And a rush of girlish fancies gave her heart a new unrest.
"Oh, the emptiness of living!" she was murmuring, soft and low,
"When the object of her being one has never come to know!

"I have mastered all my studies and have taken a degree—
I have traveled in all countries that had anything for me;
I have toiled with facts and fancies, and have turned them inside out;
But I cannot solve the problem—What this world is all about!
When I enter life in earnest, must I drone along the way
In the same old humdrum fashion that mother does today?

"If my hands a deed could compass that the soul of man would cheer!
If I could but speak a sentence that the noisy world would hear!
If I only could be rated as a hero in a strife,
Or could draw a soul from bondage, or could save a human life!
I would feel myself requited for a world of toil and pain;
I would vow that I was happy, and that life was not in vain!"

As she spoke, a mimic sailor clove the lake, not far away:
He was young, and strong, and handsome, with a fondness for display;

'Twas a gallant tourist-student, clad in mountain-climbing suit;
And he raised his cap politely, with a graceful, kind salute.
But the sudden move capsized him; and he frantic efforts made
To learn swimming in one lesson—then he loudly called for aid.

And the treacherous boat escaped him and went drifting from his clasp,
And he raised his hands in horror, without e'en a straw to grasp;
And again for help he shouted; then retreated 'neath the wave;
Then appeared again, and pleaded for a friendly hand to save.
Then the girl, with heart swift-beating, rushing to the lakelet's brim,
Said, "My chance has come: thank Heaven that a girl has learned to swim!"

And she sprang into the water, and her arms with vigor plied,
And 'twas not so many minutes ere she hovered at his side;
And she bent her shapely shoulder to his eager, trembling hand,
And went swimming toward the safety of the help-deserted land.
But a sturdy breeze came sweeping from the rude, unfriendly shore,
And the cold wind pressed against her, and her strength availed no more.

Then she struggled—oh, how bravely! but her efforts were in vain:
And she kept above the water—but no vantage could she gain;
And she prayed to God in Heaven, hoping He might lend an ear;
But Heaven seemed so far above her, and destruction was so near!
And she wildly gazed to shoreward, with a weak, despairing cry;
But no help appeared in answer, and it seemed that one must die.

And the struggling man looked at her, and then whispered in her ear,
"You can reach the shore in safety, if you only leave me here;
It were better one should perish than that death should capture two;
You have risked your life to save me—I will give my life for you.
You have shown yourself a heroine; you have done your best to save!"
Then he loosed his hold upon her, and was sinking in the wave.

Then a thousand thoughts were darting through her peril-quickened brain,
And sweet home and friends and parents stood before her, clear and plain;
And she saw the joys and pleasures that had lingered at her feet,
And life empty seemed no longer—it was wondrous dear and sweet!
And the question flashed upon her—and the answer were a strife—
"Shall I leave this man behind me in the hope to save my life?"

"IT WAS MORNING 'MONGST THE HILL-TOPS"

Songs of the Nation.

GREATER AMERICA.

Greater America—stronger America—
  Wide as the world thy beneficent fame;
Child of the earth's grandest struggle for liberty—
  Hope ever smiles at the sound of thy name!
Greater America—wider America—
  Ever the stronger and ever the same!

Thou hast of rivers that far and unceasingly
  Through the wide valleys of opulence flow;
Thou hadst of deserts that diligent husbandry
  Turned to the richest of gardens that grow!
Greater America—richer America—
  Many a summer thy harvest shall glow!

Thou hast of mountains, with snow-knitted canopies
  Pierced by the rocks that to heaven aspire;
Thou hast volcanoes—new torchlights of liberty—
  Sending the cold waves a message of fire.
Greater America—brighter America—
  Thou art the flame of the patriot's desire!

Thou hast of lakes that in sweetest tranquillity
  Lie as if sky upon earth were at rest;
Thou hast two oceans, with many an argosy
  Seeking thy shores from the East and the West.
Greater America—prouder America—
  Thou by the earth and the ocean art blest!

Thou art the world's latest refuge from tyranny—
  Out of the shadows they hurried to thee;
Now does thy hand, that has brightened their destiny,
  Carry good news to the isles of the sea.

Greater America—kinder America—
  Still art thou teaching the world to be free!

Thou hast of soldiers whose hearts beat in loyalty—
  Trained in the pride of their forefathers grand;
Ask of the foe that has tested their bravery,
  How they can fight for their own cherished land!
Greater America—fiercer America—
  Thou hast thy millions of men at command!

Thou hast of sailors whose warships of majesty
  Plough through the waves at thy every behest;
Deep is their cannons' far-echoing melody,
  Chanting the liberty-song of the West.
Greater America—prouder America—
  Now of the pride of the ocean possessed!

Thou hast of hearts that will fight for thee faithfully,
  Calling thee ever their loved and their own;
Patron of order and teacher of liberty,
  E'er with the blessings of liberty strown—
Greater America—truer America—
  Grandest of nations earth ever has known!

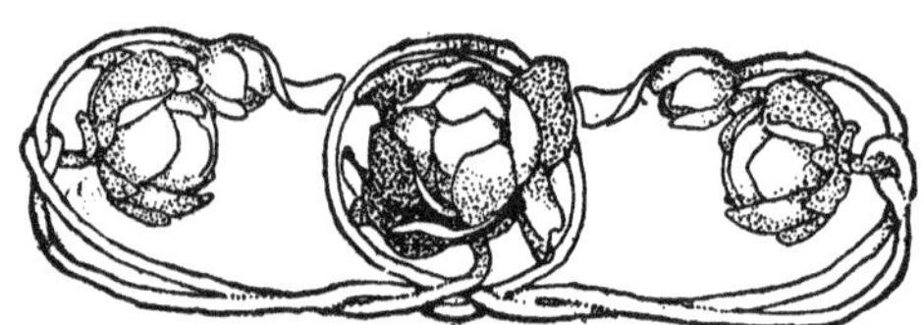

SONG—LANGUAGE OF THE FLAG.

O stars of our flag one by one you arose,
  'Till the sky on our banner was blazing with splendor!
Each ray from their depths is a night to our foes,
  And a sunburst of joy to the gallant defender.
Not only their worth cheers the land of your birth,
But flings its clear light to the ends of the earth!
And the nation shall never from victory rest,
'Till the world is as free as the Land of the West!

O stripes of the flag!—you are emblems of woe
  That fell on the hearts of the founders we cherish;
'Gainst the frowns of the storm and the guns of the foe
  They fought that the land of their love should not perish.
The stripes that gleam red are from blood that was shed,
And the white ones between are from shrouds of our dead;
And farther and farther this emblem shall wave,
'Till the world has forgot that there e'er was a slave!

O staff of our flag!—you are sturdy and strong,
  Like the people whose hands and whose hearts must uphold you!
You cling to the colors, through tempests of wrong,
  Or when 'mid the zephyrs of peace they enfold you.
On many a field, you have scorned e'er to yield,
For the hearts of the brave were your sword and your shield;
And you promise for ages to stay in your might,
'Till the world gathers round you—firm standard of right!

SONG—WESTERLAND.

Between the oceans deep and wide,
Westerland, O Westerland,
Are many nations side by side,
Westerland, O Westerland!
The waves that greet thy rocky shore,
And tell thy triumphs o'er and o'er,
Say thou shalt live forevermore,
Westerland, O Westerland!

From many mountains, broad and high,
Westerland, O Westerland,
Thy face is lifted toward the sky,
Westerland, O Westerland!
The storms that leap from hill to hill,
The lightning-bolts that dart and thrill,
But make thy people stronger still,
Westerland, O Westerland!

From prairies rich and golden mines,
Westerland, O Westerland,
Thy wealth in constant splendor shines,
Westerland, O Westerland!
The wealth that God has given to thee,
That thou a power for good might be,
And teach the nations to be free,
Westerland, O Westerland!

May all thy ways be just and pure,
Westerland, O Westerland!
That thou through ages mayst endure,
Westerland, O Westerland!
Till, emblem of the free and brave,
O'er Tyranny's dishonored grave,
Thy flag around the world shall wave,
Westerland, O Westerland!

NEW ENGLAND'S HOME-CALL.

O children, my children, where'er you may be,
From your far-scattered dwellings come home once
to me!
If you live upon mountains where valor was born,
Do they catch the first glimpse of America's morn?
If you delve in the prairie's horizon-fenced field,
Has it comelier fruits than my valleys can yield?
If pictures of splendor your cities have wrought,
Have not their strong frames from the hillsides been
brought?
If you search in the mines for the wealth that is dear,
The precious gold-dust of your kindred is here;
If temples of learning loom fair on your view,
The little old school-house is waiting for you.
With motherly pride still the children I greet,
As they rush from the door in their coverless feet,
Or learn the book-lessons of life, one by one,
The same as a Greeley and Webster have done.
Do you kneel in cathedrals?—but do not forget
That the staid Doric meeting-house prays for you yet.
The grasses still bend with the worshipping breeze,
The robins have singing-pews up in the trees;
And saints that are dead, still to earth-loves akin,
Thrill the souls of the people that worship within.
O children, dear children, where'er you may dwell,

In mountain or hillside or valley or dell,
Or island oases in deserts of sea,
O children, my children, come home once to me!

Which one of her own can a mother forget?
My heart is not granite: I long for you yet.
Come back to the past! there are still at my feet
The honest delights that make memory sweet:
The asters and golden-rods stay with their bloom,
The roses are breathing their gentle perfume;
The thistle yet blushes ere flying its seed,
The clematis clings—gleaming snow-drift of weed.
The wild-cherries ripen; the sumac-tree turns;
Like emeralds in air swing the maidenhair ferns.
The alder is hidden by clusters of vine,
The birch waxes pale at the march of the pine,
The willow the wrongs of the forest yet grieves,
And the elm clambers straight to its branches and
leaves.
The song-sparrow came from his bright summer nest,
The eagle, brave cloud-mountaineer, is my guest;
The lark sings his swift-speeding hymn to the sun,
And the whippoorwill laughs when the daylight is
done.
Sweet mosses are flocking on bowlder and tree;
O children, my children, come home once to me!

Did I fondle in tempests your first feeble wail?
Did I rock you asleep to the song of the gale?
Did I linger by windows of cottages low,
And cover your couches with blankets of snow?
Did I bar you from Nature's unlimited store,
Till you knocked with bare knuckles of toil at her
door?
Did I temper like steel in a scythe-blade your wills,
And set in your blood the clear grit of the hills?
Did I teach you Economy's dignified craft,
Withholding the weakness of Luxury's draught?
I was handing you hardships you one day would
bless,

I was planting your youth with the seeds of success;
I was giving your natures a climate of worth
That would bend to their will any climate on earth.
'Twas the training that nurtures the thrifty and free;
O children, my children, come home once to me!

From my watch-towers of hills I have viewed you afar,
Wherever the toils of humanity are;
And the waves, as they rushed for a moment to greet
The mountain-bred beaches that lie at my feet,
Have sung of my daughters and sons, o'er and o'er,
That landed wherever the sea has a shore.
No moment forget I the love and the worth
Of my children yet dwelling in halls of their birth,
Not deeming those less who in valley and hill
Stay home with the parent and comfort her still,
And who high on their mountains keep trimmed and in view
Bright torches of welcome that glisten for you;
But never a mother, by night or by day,
Can hush the heart's call for the child that's away!
Come back to the firesides! come back to the groves!
To woods in which Memory is lost as she roves!
Bring back the old songs that so linger you near,
You sing them in accents no other can hear;
Bring back the quaint stories of hillside and glen,
That laugh themselves over again and again;
Bring back the rude legends of struggle and woe;
Bring back all the joys of the sweet long ago!
My heart is not granite; I long you to see;
O children, my children, come home once to me!

THE MARCH OF THE VOLUNTEERS.

They marched their ways through the sunlit days—
  A pageant bright and strong;
Oh many a word of cheer they heard
  From many a crowded throng!
'Twas the orator's cry, "You pencil high
  In letters of gold each name:
As you walk the streets to loud drum-beats,
  You are climbing the hills of fame!"
'Twas the matron's cry, "There is suffering nigh,
  To furrow the laurelled brow;
But never was yet a mother's debt
  More splendidly paid than now!"
'Twas the maiden's cry, "It is sweet to die
  For the country's sake, 'tis said;
But be you true, my lover in blue,
  I will love you alive or dead!"

They marched their ways in the bright spring days
  Past statues great and tall
Of the country's pride, who had lived or died
  And given the land their all.
And Lincoln seemed to the heart that dreamed,
  From his chiselled lips to speak:
"The mission of might should be to fight
  For those that are crushed and weak!"
And Grant spoke loud to the marching crowd,
  "Make heavy and hard your blows;
The shortest way to a peaceful day
  Is over a field of foes!"
And Fame's star-son, our Washington,
  Spoke then from his kingless throne,
"You are heart and hand with the greatest land
  That ever the world has known!"

DO NOT FORGET THE WOUNDED.

Now, in the days of triumph, when victory's golden bells
Sweep like a song of gladness over the hills and dells,
Do not forget the wounded—the almost worse than slain,
Waging a fight, by day and night, with the slow, grim enemy—Pain!

Now, when the cities are safer because of their battles grand,
Now, when the mountains are sweeter because there is peace in the land,
Do not forget the sick men—lying in misery there,
Who made their fight for God and the right, in that blazing tropical glare!

Far from their home and kindred—far from the joys of life,
Far from the restful soothing of mother, sister, or wife,
Alone because they were noble, in agony's fearful clutch—
Is there a gem too bright for them, or a help that costs too much?

Jewels and satins and laces—how sweetly they gleam above
The cherished forms and faces of those that we know and love!
But what were all of their splendor, if dimmed with deadly fear?
If fortress and town were beaten down, and the Spanish hosts were here?

Oh, it was grand and glorious to get the news of peace,
When from the Chief came sounding the words that war might cease;
Glad were the welcome tidings that sped o'er valley and hill;
But the wounds that were made by fever and blade, are aching and bleeding still!

Greet the returning heroes and trim their pathway grand:
There's ne'er too good a gift for those who fight for their native land!
Honor to all the boys in blue and make their coming bright,
But never forget the heavy debt we owe to the boys in white!

THE PASSING OF THE MOTHER.

Mary A. Bickerdyke—War-Nurse.

Through the wide reach of Eternity's portals
Marched an unbroken procession of mortals:
Held through the clouds and the sunlight their way—
Those who had "died" on that day.
Each was to each near as sister or brother;
Pauper and millionaire jostled each other;
Jewels and money the dying might save;
Beauty was left in the grave.

Out of Death's mystery-moment of slumber,
Warriors and potentates came, without number.
Many the friends of the past they were meeting!
But there was heard no tumultuous greeting,
Till came a woman, with days fully told—
Wrinkled and weary and old.

Then the great news traversed all of those regions;
Then came a rally of swift-footed legions;
Making with plaudits the path all aglow,
Down which this woman must go.
Ne'er were the honors she lingered between,
Paid to a king or a queen!
Not with grim tools of the death-dealing labor;
Not with presenting of musket or saber;
But by an edge of the fame-bordered street,
Knelt every man at her feet.

Then said those soldiers, in accents caressing,
"Mother, O Mother, your glance and your blessing:
Well may that luxury thrill with delight—

Make even Heaven more bright!"
Then said the woman, "My heroes, 'tis done:
Rise to your feet, every one.
Nought in my work was of grandeur or beauty:
Love was my countersign—Help was my duty."

Then said a soldier, "I lay on a meadow,
Scythed by fierce battle—then garnered in shadow.
Night's gloomy sepulchre gathered around me;
Man had deserted and God had not found me.
'Let the dead rest', said my comrades, in sorrow:
'Then to Earth's arms we will give them tomorrow.'
And the dead rested: but I, partly slain,
Watched with my murderous pain.
Then my weak lips could not utter a word—
Only a groan; but 'twas heard!
Heard by one heart through the sulphurous distance—
Heart that was toiling for others' existence.
How like a star to my life's eager craving,
Looked the rude lantern she bore to my saving;
How she brought back to me Earth's vanished charms—
Lifting me there in her arms!
Tell me, O comrades: and is it not meet
That I should bow at her feet?"

Then said a soldier, "The North-wind was sweeping
Down through the Sun-land: its white blades were reaping
Harvests of death; and the torn tents were falling
In that new tempest of bleakness appalling.
Men full of deeds fit for Spartan or Roman
Shrank from the charge of our frost-crested foeman
Bidding defiance to sword and to gun—
Scorning the earth and the sun.
'Moscow-retreat', thought both timid and brave—
'Not into France—but the grave.'
Oh, but all valor had proved unavailing,
But for our Mother's swift courage unfailing!

Joan of Arc 'gainst this enemy pallid,
Gaily her hosts of resistance she rallied.
Soon from her warm heart so dauntless though tender,
Sprang a huge campfire unrivalled in splendor:
Even the ramparts she, fearless of blame,
Stole, for the life-giving flame.
'Under arrest' for that glorious robbing,
Still was her great soul with sympathy throbbing;
Convict of red-tape, proud pris'ner heroic,
Heart of a Christian and nerves of a Stoic,
Hailed she the conflict, and entered upon it:
Fought a campaign 'gainst Destruction—and won it;
Charged with her might on the cohorts of Grief—
Gave every suf'ring relief.
Many a poor boy, in homesickness dumb,
Felt that his mother had come!—
We who had died had she reckoned without us,
There in those graves that were freezing about us,
But for the hardship and blame that she bore,
Who would have done for us more?
What though she signal me frowns as I tell it:
Who but our God could excel it?"

Then said a soldier, "My life-blood was flowing;
Into the future this sad soul was going.
Darkest of robes my crushed spirit was wearing!
What had I left, but eternal despairing?
Then to the scene this evangelist brought
Prayers that my parents had taught;
Then with sweet hymns she my anguish beguiled—
Hymns I had loved when a child.
Then did this saint, with fond eyes bending o'er,
Sing of the sweet 'Shining Shore';
Then came the Land of the Blest to my seeing;
Then a bright future pervaded my being;
Then did the pangs of my pain cease to cumber;
Then did I glide into blisses of slumber.
Slept with that soul-thrilling voice in my ear,

Full of enchantment and cheer;
Slept till I journeyed from Night into Day,
Dreaming that song all the way.
So did she soothe me as could but one other—
Sanctified Sister and Mother!"

Then came the Christ of Humanity: saying,
"Daughter, thy crown; I, my Father obeying,
Gladly this token of glory bring nigh,
Gleaming with stars of the sky.
Stars of all magnitudes flash, as thou waitest:
All hast thou blessed—from the least to the greatest."
Then said the woman, "O Master of Mission!
Hear thee, I pray thee, a humble petition:
Let me work on, my vocation pursuing:
Nought have I done to what yet needs the doing.
Stow this sweet gift in some worthier place,
While I still toil for my race!"

THE ABSENT SOLDIER'S CHILD.

By the dusty roadway wand'ring,
Came I to a garden fair;
Spendthrift flowers were gaily squand'ring
Sweets upon the summer air.

Trained and trellised vines sedately
Nursed their buds to blossoms bright;
Trees were standing, tall and stately,
In the sunbeams' mellow light.

Lacked my lovely garden only
Human forms, to perfect be:—
Brightest spots grow dull and lonely,
When but one there is to see.

Look! there comes a tiny maiden,
From an angle of the wall,
With a score of flow'rets laden
(She the fairest of them all);

To a shapely mound, low-clinging
In that garden's choicest nook,
This young maiden, softly singing,
All her blossomed riches took.

With a bound, I stood before her:
"Why is this, my little maid?"
Soft I whispered, bending o'er her;
She was shy, but not afraid.

In her eyes a teardrop glistened,
  In her voice were thrills of love;
And I worshipped while I listened
  As to angels from above:

"Papa far away is sleeping
  With some soldier-friends," she said:
"He is in his Saviour's keeping;
  But we cannot find his bed.

"Yes, in Heaven his soul is living!
  But it makes him seem more near,
If I, flow'rets to him giving,
  'Make believe' that he is here."

A SONG FOR OUR FLEETS.

A song for our fleets—our iron fleets
Of grim and savage beauty,
That plough their way through fields of spray,
To follow a nation's duty!
The winds may blow and the waves may flow
And stars may hide their faces,
But little we reck; our stars o'er-deck
Still glitter within their places!

Let never a one who gazes on
This pageant calm but splendid,
Doubt that our coasts from hostile hosts
Will gallantly be defended!
A desperate foe may wish us woe;
But what is their petty knavery
Against the right, when backed with might
And Anglo-Saxon bravery?

A song for our fleets—our gallant fleets,
'Neath flags of glory flying,
That carried the aid, so long delayed,
To those that were crushed and dying!
And flames might glow, and blood might flow;
But still, with a stern endeavor,
We ruled the main, and lashed foul Spain
From our Western world forever!

"—OUR IRON FLEETS,
OF GRIM AND SAVAGE BEAUTY"

GRIDLEY.

Not till the fight was done,
Not till the last fierce gun
  Startled the wave,
Didst thou, at Death's low call,
Turning thy back to all,
  Sail for the grave.

Glory withheld till now
Gleamed on thy modest brow,
  'Mid plaudits grand;
Warrior of ocean, we
Waited with wreaths for thee
  In thine own land.

Those that thou lovedst were here,
Yearning till thou wast near
  To tell their pride;
Through many an ocean-storm,
Hearts ever fond and warm
  Sailed by thy side.

True as thy ship's good steel,
Hiding, with Spartan zeal,
  The murderous pain,
In ocean's grandest fight
Thy hand was first to smite
  The brow of Spain.

Firmer than mountain-rocks
That breast the storm-cloud shocks—
  With courage proud

Didst thou on fury's track
Iron thunderbolts hurl back,
    And rend the cloud.

Not till thy fame's bright star
Had pierced the mists of war,
    And glittered high,
Did thy choice spirit turn,
And, higher rank to earn,
    Seek the blue sky.

COMIN' BACK TO 'PELIER.

Vermont Farmer's Version.

Dewey's comin! load the anvils! fill the welcome-cup!
Comin' back to 'Pelier, whar he hed his bringin' up;
Comin' from the torrid zone, an' the battle's brunt—
Fetchin' us a history—his pictur' way in front!
Wabblin' under praises more than he can count,
An' goin' to bring the whole thing back to old Varmount!
Yes, they'll try to spile him, when he gits as fur as 'York:
Give him linen napkins, an' a silver knife an' fork;
Speechin' him an' preachin' him, an' tryin' to explain
Somethin' that he knows already—how he walloped Spain;
Showin' him the Brooklyn Bridge in reg'lar welcome-trim,
Tryin' to make out, p'rhaps, they built it all for him;
Feedin' him on china, for his breakfas', dine, an' sup;
But you wait till he's in 'Pelier, where he hed his bringin'-up!

Yes, it's somethin', these here honors thankful people give,
In the towns an' counties whar he didn't use to live;
Nothin', you will see, though, the hearts of townsmen melts,
Like a townsman's honors he hez picked up somewhar else!
Ain't no room fur jealousy, when they thus advance:
"All of us c'u'd done the same, ef we'd hed a chance!"
Let 'em give him gilded houses, fur a splendid prison:
But when he lands in 'Pelier, all the village will be his'n!

Folks'll come from all p'ints—a hundred miles may be,
To view the hill-bred sailor that is hero of the sea;
Island-born an' prairie-born the contrac' often fills,
But fur somethin' more'n unusual, try the everlastin' hills!

Men'll turn their backs to the mountains fur to see him,
Boys'll sprout ambition, an'll wish that they could be him;
Ol' maids they will wonder how they ever came to miss him,
Galls'll sort o' flutter, an'll wish that they could kiss him.
Ol' Seth Warner's honored ghost'll haste to see the show,
Brave Remember Baker'll be among the first to go;
An' it's tol'ble certain, that before the spree is done,
Colonel Ethan Allen'll be up from Burlin'ton.
But George won't turkey 'roun' no more, I'll bet ye, ten to one,
Than in days when he wa'n't nothin' 'ceptin' Ol' Doc Dewey's son.

Dewey's comin'—fire the anvils! drain the welcome-cup!
Comin' down to 'Pelier, whar he hed his bringin'-up;
Dewey's comin'! wave the banners! string 'em all about!
Comin' down to 'Pelier, whar he form'ly started out;
Bringin' new geogeraphies, a year or less in age,
That's got his pictur', true as life, right on the openin' page!

IN THE WRECKAGE OF THE MAINE.

In the farm-lands or the city
  Grieves a woman—sad—alone;
'Neath God's everlasting pity
  She is weeping for her own.
Cabinets have toiled and wrangled,
  Statesmen could not soothe her pain—
For that weary heart is tangled
  In the wreckage of the Maine.

Through the golden halls of fashion
  Moves a lady tall and fair;
Round her gleam the flames of passion
  On the soft magnetic air.
Suitors bow and bend above her,
  But their wiles are all in vain:
She is thinking of a lover
  In the wreckage of the Maine.

On a cot, the sailor lying
  Rests his soul in silent prayer;
Through the long days he is dying;
  But his tears are falling there
For the gallant fellow-seamen
  Who will rest, while Time shall reign,
In that sepulchre of freemen,
  'Neath the wreckage of the Maine.

On a continent of splendor
  Is a nation calmly grand—
Freedom's natural defender—
  Honest labor's helping hand:
And it speaks, half kind, half cruel:
  "Liberty, O haughty Spain,
Soon may grasp another jewel
  From the wreckage of the Maine!"

CUBA TO COLUMBIA.

Published in April, 1896.

A voice went over the waters—
 A stormy edge of the sea—
Fairest of Freedom's daughters,
 Have you no help for me?
Do you not hear the rusty chain
 Clanking about my feet?
Have you not seen my children slain,
 Whether in cell or street?
Oh, if you were sad as I,
 And I as you were strong,
You would not have to call or cry—
 You would not suffer long!

"Patience"?—have I not learned it,
 Under the crushing years?
Freedom—have I not earned it,
 Toiling with blood and tears?
"Not of you?"—my banners wave
 Not on Egyptian shore,
Or by Armenia's mammoth grave—
 But at your very door!
Oh, if you were needy as I,
 And I as you were strong,

You should not suffer, bleed, and die,
  Under the hoofs of wrong!

Is it that you have never
  Felt the oppressor's hand,
Fighting, with fond endeavor,
  To cling to your own sweet land?
Were you not half dismayed,
  There in the century's night,
Till to your view a sister's aid
  Came, like a flash of light?
Oh, what gift could ever be grand
  Enough to pay the debt,
If out of the starry Western land,
  Should come my Lafayette!

COLUMBIA TO CUBA.

Written May 21, 1902.

A voice went over the waters—
  The edge of a sunlit sea—
Newest of Freedom's daughters,
  My help went out to thee.
Time it was that the West should aid
  A sister of the West,
When her own mother's jewelled blade
  Was stabbing at her breast!
Where in battle my bullets flew
  Along your gallant shore,
Much indeed I was aiding you—
  But Civilization more!

Patience?—yes, you have learned it:
  And, now, 'neath Freedom's sky,
See that you have not spurned it,
  As years go hurrying by.
Yes!—we are dwelling side by side,
  Ready for clasp or thrust:
Long may this friendship be our pride,
  Fruiting to love and trust.
You to keep the rescued land
  Still to the rescuer true—

" NEWEST OF FREEDOM'S DAUGHTERS,
MY HELP WENT OUT TO THEE '

We to vow that Tyranny's hand
  Never shall fall on you!

If to your glance my starry flame
  Looks like a welcome bright,
Cherish the thought from which it came,
  In your ambition's sight.
Do not on the horizon rest—
  Do not sink below:
Rise, O new-born star of the West,
  Unto meridian glow!
Climb to OUR constellation
  That all earth awes and cheers,
And—nation within a nation—
  Gleam bright for a thousand years!

COLLOQUY OF GRIEF.

William McKinley died September 14, 1901.

Nation bright with the sunrise-glow—
  Full of the century's throbbing—
Why do you bow your head so low?
  Why do we hear you sobbing?........
Death has climbed to my highest place,
And tears of a people are no disgrace;
Sorrow is better told than kept;
And grief is holy, for God has wept.

Nation with banner of oldest birth,
  Stars to the high stars sweeping,
Why have you not a flag on earth,
  But to the half-mast creeping?........
Many a brave man had to die,
To hold those colors against the sky;
Agonies such as this reveal
That every banner to Heaven must kneel!

Nation with tasks that might appal
  Planets of weak endeavor,
Why did the best man of you all
  Sail from your shores forever?........
Not forever and not from sight,
But nearer to God's sweet kindly light:
Through the mists to a stormless sea,
Where all the heroes of ages be.

Nation with weapons fierce and grim,
  Sharpen with rage your sadness:
Tear the murderer limb from limb—
  Torture him into madness!........
No! I have Heaven too much in awe,

The law to avenge with lack of law:
Take we the soul from its tainted clod,
And lay it down at the feet of God.

Nation whose love for home ne'er dies,
  Cruel the clouds that hover!
What do you say when a woman cries,
  "Give me my husband-lover?"........
Sad heart, carry the grievous wrong
In Faith's own arms; it will not be long.
Here, and in lands you never knew,
He more than ever will comfort you.

Nation of many tribes and lands—
  Strength of the world's best nations,
Say! would a million murderous hands
  Crumble your deep foundations?........
Never! no poison e'er can blight
The flowers and fruitage of truth and right;
Never! the land that the tyrant fears,
Shall live in splendor a thousand years!

A MAN HAS DIED.

September 14, 1901.

A man has died—and so have myriads more—
  They will, while yet this dying earth lives on;
But when a leader makes the utmost shore,
  We sadly look toward where his ship has gone,
And only get this message from the dead:
"Study the past: my words have all been said."

A woman mourns—as woman always must,
  So long as joy has penalties of pain;
How sadly creeps that sweet soul in the dust!
  And yet her fearful woe is not in vain:
It teaches us that though love long endure,
Only in Heaven its raptures are secure.

THE VICTORY-WRECK.

O stealthily-creeping Merrimac,
  Hush low your fiery breath:
You who gave life to ships of strife
  Are sailing unto your death!—
"I am ready and dressed for burial,
  Beneath the Cuban wave;
But still I can fight for God and right,
  While resting in my grave!"

O men that are sailing the Merrimac,
  Your hearts are beating high;
But send a prayer through the smoking air,
  To your Captain in the sky!—
"We know there is death in every breath,
  As we cling to the gunless deck;
And grand will be our voyage, if we
  Can make of our ship a wreck!"

Now drop the bower of the Merrimac,
  And swing her with the tide.
Now scuttle her, braves, and bid the waves
  Sweep into her shattered side!—
"Through a flying hell of shot and shell,
  We passed Death, with a sneer;
We wrenched our life from the novel strife,
  And even our foemen cheer!"

LIBERTY'S TORCH.

Out of the east comes a maiden
  Over the rough stormy sea,
Full of good gifts for us laden—
  Love from the free to the free.
Now with her torch brightly glowing,
  In our chief gateway she stands,
Liberty's radiance throwing
  Over the seas and the lands.

Men by their firesides wherever
  News of the world is a guest,
Talk of the gift and the giver—
  Know of our star in the west.
Even the ancient defenders
  Cannot this symbol forget:
Washington knows of its splendors—
  So does the proud Lafayette.

Tell me, O well-studied scholars
  Of the world's glory and shame,
Now should a few paltry dollars
  Spoil this beneficent flame?
Ask of our friends and our foemen,
  Ask of our hopes and our doubt—

Can we withstand the dread omen
  EVER to see it go out?

Let not our colors be fading!
  Let not a sceptre and crown—
Let not the triumphs of trading—
  Trample our sentiment down!
Ice-blooded tyranny, listen!
  Patriots, we laugh at your fears!
Liberty's emblem shall glisten
  Yet for a thousand of years!

SONGS OF PLEASURE AND PAIN.

FARMER STEBBINS AWHEEL.

I went to Brooklyn visitin' to see what I could see,
An' twenty thousan' bicycles come rushin' after me;
I couldn't even cross the road, or stop to look around,
But some one's wheel was sure to want that very inch of ground;
An' those at whom I shook my fist at scarin' of me thus
Would call me names an' skitter off, 'fore I could clinch the fuss.

An' some of them was double-bent, with noses near the ground,
As if their pocketbooks was lost, an' hadn't yet been found;
An' some was steamin' 'long the road, in reg'lar engine-shape,
As if they'd stole a dollar-bill, an' wanted to escape;
An' some was wildly chewin' gum, industrious as could be,
As if they'd lately took a job to gnaw a hemlock tree;

An' some had faces of despair, as if on frenzy's brink,
An' some was men an' some was boys, an' some was girls—I think;
An' some was ladies lady-dressed, an' lookin' fine an' neat
As that same number of bouquets a-glidin' down the street;
An' when a man about my size come ridin' with a dame,
I says, "If he can pump a wheel, then I can do the same."

A little boy with turn-up nose an' unregenerate eye
Had overheard my loud remarks, an' told the followin' lie:
He says to me, "The cycles all have big improvements, now,
An' any one can ride 'em though he hasn't first learned how";
An' so I hired a stout machine from some one in a store,
An' mounted on, an' started off the village to explore.

The snub-nose boy he helped me up with all the strength he had,
Then give a push, an' hollered out, "A pleasant journey, Dad!"

An' so it was, a rod or two; when, like some livin' dunce,
The lean an' slippery critter tried to go two ways at once;
An' like a polertician-chap, I strove to do the same,
An' felt the ground reverberate beneath my massive frame.

I looked around to find the boy: he wasn't nowhere seen,
An' I raised up the bicycle, a-feelin' rather green;
An' then I said, "There's some mistake; I'll try the thing ag'in,
An' it will probably behave, when I have broke it in."
An' so I leaped upon its back, an' started off once more;
An' promptly felt the earth ag'in, through all the clothes I wore.

An' then I sort o' twisted 'round, an' rose into a rage,
An' started wildly in once more, the critter to engage;
An' hollered loud, so all the folks come runnin' 'round to see,
"You little beast, you think you'll get the upper han's of me?
Perhaps you think a farmer bold hain't pluck to bring you down,
That's broke some thirty colts to bit, an' half the mules in town!"

An' then I strove for victory, with all my varied powers,
For ten good minutes by the clock, but seemin'ly for hours;
An' every time I made a move my mastery to display,
The little wretch would twist itself in some new-fashioned way;
An' sometimes it would lie an' rest, as placid as could be,
Then I'd be on my back, an' it a-grinnin' down at me;

An' then 'twould rear up like a horse, an' weave an' twist awhile,
An' I would stan' upon my head, in reg'lar circus-style;
An' then 'twould kind o' paw the earth, an' wave its hinder wheel,
An' I would turn a somerset, and give a frenzied squeal;
Until at last I laid amongst a million laughin' folks,
My head upon a pavin'-stone—my legs between some spokes;

An' shouted, as I give my neck a slow an' painful turn,
"Bring me that snub-nose boy that said we didn't have to learn!
Give me the man that first among a trustin' people came
An' set at large this dang'rous beast with 'Safety' for its name!
I'll whip 'em with each other in as good a shape, you'll see,
As this 'ere bunch of metal bones has threshed the earth with me!"

THE FUNERAL-EXPRESS.

See what from the town approaches,
With its stately line of coaches,
With its engine-jewels gleaming
In the sunlight o'er them streaming:
'Tis the funeral-train!
In its rooms so swiftly flying,
There are hundreds slowly dying:
Yet they mark with curious pity
Some who in the painless city
Will forget their pain.

In those halls so swiftly flying,
There is moaning, there is crying,
For the wreckage that reposes
'Neath the lilies and the roses
Of the funeral-train.
Some are leisure-hours beguiling,
Unaware, amid their smiling,
Of the burials of the morrow,
That will rush with equal sorrow,
Through *their* heart and brain!

In that hearse so swiftly flying,
Is an old man, meekly lying;
Eighty harvests fell upon him,
Ere the silent sickle won him
From the standing grain;
And, with frozen smile and dimple,
Lies a babe, divinely simple,
Who, before this world discerning,
Found itself to God returning,
With no earthly stain.

In that tomb so swiftly flying,
Is a face the world defying,
Manhood's guise, in beastly fashion:
Just a page of reckless passion
  Love implored in vain;
And a girlish one of sweetness,
Yet with womanhood's completeness,
And a semblance always thrilling,
Death could not succeed in killing,
  When her heart was slain.

In that crypt so swiftly flying,
Now a marble mansion nighing,
  Is a corse arrayed in splendor—
Wealth its pitiful defender,
  Death a doubtful gain;
And another that must grovel
In The Acre's humblest hovel,
Yet with tears and sorrow nigh him
Such as money ne'er could buy him,
  Shares the funeral-train.

Now this throng of strange appearing
Death's wide palace-door is nearing:
With his subjects round him lying,
Only earthly king undying,
  Long has been his reign!
Pride and power cannot ignore him;
All must cast themselves before him;
Journeys, whether mean or splendid,
Shall forever here be ended:
  Stop the funeral-train.

TOOK JOHNNIE TO THE SHOW.

Poor little Johnnie longed to go
And see the show;
Like any simple trusting lad
Who viewed the walls in pictures clad,
Of men who lived on horses' backs,
Or climbed each other's heads in stacks,
Or drivelled dressed in stripes and spots,
Or tied themselves in double knots,
Or metamorphosed into wheels,
Or swung each other by the heels,
Or, placid, led unblemished lives
Amid a fusillade of knives,
Or punched the lion while he roared,
Or with their heads his mouth explored:—
You would yourself have longed to go
And see the show!

Then Johnnie's father said, "Although
I loathe, abhor, and hate the show,
I feel that little John should go,
  The curious animals to see;
'Twould never do—so little grown—
For him to wander round alone:
  My little boy shall go with me."
And Johnnie's mother—prudent dame—
And Johnnie's auntie, felt the same;
And Johnnie's Uncle Lemuel,
His second cousin, Samuel,
His older sister, Mary,
And Susan Ann and Sarah,

His brother and his brotherinlaw,
His father's cautious motherinlaw,
And others, went along with him
To see that nought was wrong with him;
'Twas not a sin to take, you know,
Poor Johnnie to the show!

As any one might be afraid,
'Twas very hard, with all this aid,
  For little John to see the show.
They hustled him, they jostled him,
  They pulled him to and fro;
When one of them would chance to see
A knot of friends, then he or she
Would grasp the urchin by the hand,
So all the world would understand
That they had simply come, you know,
  With Johnnie to the show.
And Johnnie's heart was breaking,
His lengthened arms were aching,
His pulse was wildly throbbing,
His little breath was sobbing,
When with a new and different ache
  In every separate toe,
He lay at night—in his own charge—
  A dreary poor and lonely one,
  And murmured, "I'm the only one
Of all the family, small or large,
  That didn't see the show!"

381.

Who is this man they bury today,
  Out of the cheerful sun?
"He was a 'cop,' " I heard them say;
"That was his number, by the way—
  381."

That is his helmet, on the pall,
  There is his belt, undone;
There is a wreath of flowers let fall—
Making just three figures in all—
  381.

There is a medal on his breast,
  For some brave deed done;
Still, he was not of fame possessed;
He was only, at worst and best,
  381.

Stopped a horse, once, running away,
  Saved a wife and son;
It was remembered half a day;
"Only his duty," I heard them say;
  "381."

Rushed up into a house one night
  (Danger ne'er to shun);
Dragged three children into sight,
Out of the fire; yes, that was right,
  381!

Clubbed a man, one day, half dead
  (People said "for fun");

Still, there was this much to be said:
He came near being stabbed instead—
381.

Yes, he had faults! and such as might
Your pure excellence stun;
But he was perfect in a fight;
When in trouble you loved to sight
381!

Always sought and called-for first,
When there was risk to run;
Asked for his best amid the worst—
When it was over, often cursed,
381!

Still, some threads of love and glee
Into his days were spun;
He had a wife and children three—
And they weep for him, as we see—
381!

And he had comrades, as have you—
Willingly foe to none;
And they are out, once more to view
Him that to them was ever true—
381.

Under the Great Chief let him trust,
In the new life begun;
Soul to soul, and dust to dust,
And a God that is ever just—
Now that his work is done.

TO THE CZAR.

Strange king, who in a golden cradle lying,
Awoke one morn 'mid battle-banners flying,
And wept beneath a wealth of princely naming,
And heard the cannon's death-hoarse voice proclaiming
Joy, that in spite of sly rebellion's malice,
The stork had wandered safely to the palace,
You, who amid your childhood fancies dreaming,
Were guarded by the musket-dagger's gleaming,
Whose coronation's unpreceded splendors
Were in a camp of battle-trained defenders—
Accept a Yankee scribe's congratulations
(Least from the grandest of the Western nations),
And let him say (who has no cause to fear you,
And who would talk the same words, were he near you;
And look you in the eye—that prince of senses—
With western ease as to the consequences),

Strange king, you have as authors term it lately,
Struck a new vein; and we admire you greatly.
Still, not the newness of your proclamation,
But its strange plan—enkindles admiration;
The thriftiest Quaker that may now adore you
Preached your new sermon, years and years before you,
The absent soldier's yearning wife or mother
Has seldom had a heart for any other;
The bravest captain of our time was praying
For peace, while yet his thousands grimly slaying;
E'en tyrants offer peace on one condition—

The patriot's perfect and abject submission;
But you, strange Czar, have asked the nations whether
They cannot live and strive in peace together,
A hymn of love in varied language singing
And the millennium to our doorways bringing.

O that the world may be the proud possessor
Of such, from warlike Vladimir's successor!
From one who e'en amid his childhood-stories
Was led among the camps of martial glories!
Who heard how, with devoted men around him,
The Donskoi crushed a fourfold yoke that bound
him;
Of Ivan, who in unity delighting
Made Russia peaceful by the fiercest fighting!
Of Peter, great with selfness and devotion,
Who fought and won a gateway to the ocean!
Of Catherine, who with martial tribulations
Forced Poland to become a serf of nations!
Of Moscow—city which, its star at nadir—
With costly firebrands froze the French invader;
Of Nicholas, who, scheming despot branded,
Fought three united nations single-handed!

Here is a story, famed in many dwellings,
We both have heard—though far apart the tellings:
There lived a rich man, weary, sad, and sated,
For whom, unborn, the floods of wealth had waited;
He ploughed a golden sea without endeavor,
But comfort's shore seemed out of view forever,
Until, the dictates of his heart defying,
He sent Pride's banner to the topmast flying,
And sailed, with misery throbbing for confession,
Among the palace-isles of his possession.
Now, one day, when the air was clear and tender,
He gazed into the sky's far-distant splendor,
And felt it might be ranked among the pleasures,
If he could add Heaven's wealth unto his treasures.
So, soon, a thorny rocky headland reaching,

Where Heaven's young prince the multitude was
 teaching,
He asked Heaven's price. The answer's soul is living:
"Give all thou hast, and never cease thy giving."

If you, odd Czar, Heaven's peace for earth are ask-
 ing,
And would that all beneath God's smile were bask-
 ing,
If you would gild the lot of prince and peasant,
And purchase Heaven to make our race a present,
Not only mind this mandate to the letter,
But to the spirit—which is vastly better.
Upon the gathered pride of centuries trample,
And set all men a Christ-endowed example:
Wait not an hour for other king or nation,
But feed your guns to one great conflagration;
Burn all the warlike flags that gleam about you;
Let not the waiting world a moment doubt you;
Turn all your splendors into humble kindness,
And succor human want and woe and blindness;
Let only your own friendliness befriend you;
And though there may be those who turn and rend
 you,
And though your dynasty may fall and crumble,
And though you walk the world abject and humble,
And though ingratitude with pain may fill you,
And though, alas! the world should turn and kill
 you,
One life for millions were a thrifty barter;
And God's most glorious plans require a martyr.

TO FANNY CROSBY.

Blind Hymn-Poet, Aged Eighty.

Song-bird in the dark,
Adding each day unto our lyric treasure,
And rising, like the lark,
Nearer to heaven for each ecstatic measure:

Sing on, O rich, clear voice,
'Mid the world's clamor for the world's possession;
Thou art the angels' choice
To give their sweetest anthems earth-expression!

Love on, O gentle heart,
To all mankind with stately pureness clinging;
The followers of thy art,
With lips devout caress thee in their singing!

In myriad temples grand,
Through whose broad aisles the organ-tones are pealing,
Thy words walk hand in hand
With truths the rich-bound Bible is revealing.

By many a cottage-door,
Where Faith and Love with Poverty are dwelling,
Thy sweet words, o'er and o'er,
The mother to her new-found babe is telling.

Where Arctic snow-storms sweep,
Where tropic ghosts a hand to death are reaching,
Thy jewelled words still keep
Their tryst with God, and aid His solemn teaching.

Song-bird in the light,
Thou shalt see splendors when this world's have faded!
E'en now thy path is bright
With stars in heaven whose kindling thou hast aided.

Yearn on, O lofty soul,
Though voices from the song-land intercede thee!
Spurn not this earth's control
Yet many years: our suffering mortals need thee.

But when at last The King
Shall bid thy friends above to cease their waiting,
The angels, sure, will sing,
To welcome thee, some hymn of thy creating.

And Christ will be thy guide,
Confirming, step by step, his wondrous story;
And seek the Father's side,
And say, "She taught the world to sing thy glory."

THE MAIDEN-MOTHER.

Under a Picture of the Madonna.

Fair maiden-mother!—whom-to do you pray?—
  Not to a far-off God, in pity hearing
  Proud prayers through smoke of sacrifice appearing,
And brazen bugle-songs from mouths of clay,
And priests the altars fatten day by day;
  But to the child—half loving it, half fearing—
Who brings with him from yonder star-floored place,
Heaven as a present to the human race.

Child of all nations!—has the soul within thee
  Yet told the body of its destined path?
  How it must walk through flames of human wrath,
How frantic rage to agonies will pin thee,
And fallen angels will reach up to win thee;
  How thou must reap Sin's dreary aftermath,
And, clasping to thy heart man's only loss,
Eclipse it with the glory of the cross?

THE OLD CHURCH-BELL.

We walk to church along the olden way,
We drink of peace from out the Sabbath Day;
The worldly chain has loosed its links of care,
The cry of trade has vanished from the air;
E'en yonder clouds that gather at the west
Seem templed halls for worship and for rest.
But silences awake us from our spell:
For we have lost the old church-bell—
That through the miles could send a magic voice,
And summon men to sorrow and rejoice.

We saw the bride upon her blossomed way—
With heart that beat to echoes sadly-gay,
With all the past a dream beneath her sight—
With all the future full of visions bright.
Oh blithe it was, to bow the comely head
At altars where her parents once were wed!
And yet a silence on her spirits fell:
She did not hear the old church-bell
Rejoice to know the gladness she had found,
And throw to her its golden gift of sound.

The sainted chief will enter here no more;
In coffined garb he leaves the sacred door.
Now they have wept around his solemn rest,
And, sobbing, sung the hymns he loved the best;

And gifted tongues have joined in friendly strife
To coin in words the richness of his life.
But he has missed his most befitting knell:
    They could not toll the old church-bell—
That greeted him with pure and single tongue,
And brooded o'er him when he prayed or sung.

The temple's ways are marching with the times;
And now the gilded steeple sings its chimes.
And sweet it is, upon a morning fair,
To hear our hymns go floating through the air!
And oft they reach the sick one in his bed,
And oft pursue the sinner that hath fled;
But 'twas not needful, and it was not well,
    To take away the old church-bell—
For long it stayed, a true though lofty friend,
And might have been our comrade to the end.

MONOLOGUE OF PAIN.

I am the angel, soft-hearted Pain.
  I watch over mortals as mothers might do—
I guard them, I keep them, I plan for their gain;
  My warning is speedy—my judgment is true.
I stand at the door where the death-hound, Disease,
  Hot-crazy for blood, has just scented his prey;
I rush to the victim he hastens to seize—
  I wake him, I warn him, I bid him Away!
      I am the angel—
      The dark-hued evangel—
Bringing the good news of danger to men;
      They who will heed me
      Seldom may need me;
Soon I return to my watchtower again.

I am the devil, red-handed Pain.
  I hang over mortals when helpless they lie;
I stab them, I rack them, I rend them in twain,
  Till, wearied with anguish, they pray they may die.
I lurk where the battle's red banner appears,
  I poison the wounds, and I follow the blows;
I torture the fallen, and laugh at their tears;

For I am the cruellest, fiercest of foes.
I am a devil—
A symbol of evil—
Feasting my fury on sorrows of men;
Not till Death snatches
My prey from my clutches,
Will I return to my comfortless den.

I am the monitor, chastening Pain.
I punish the mortals who do themselves wrong,
I bind them, I beat them, I leave them my stain;
My vengeance is certain—my patience is long.
I dull the keen edge of their luckless desire,
I give them true words they may cherish alway;
I burn in their memory symbols of fire,
To warn them and hold them from going astray.
Over the portals
That open for mortals,
Into the Edens where serpents creep low,
Cherubim, aiming
Their trusty blades flaming,
Place I, that mortals their dangers may know.

BICYCLE-SONG.

Oh, Bessie has bought her a bonnet of red,
  And started afoot for the ball;
She never was minding a word that I said,
  Or looking about for my call!
Quit mourning, quit mourning, good Mother, I say:
She maybe will linger to talk on the way:
I'll follow the truant as well as I may,
  And catch her, whatever befall.

Oh, Bessie has bought her a bonnet of blue,
  And started to ride to the ball;
She's taken the speediest horse that she knew,
  The swiftest that stood in the stall!
Quit mourning, good Mother, it might have been worse;
There's many a mount that is better than hers;
I'll follow her closely with saddle and purse,
  And catch her, whatever befall.

Oh, Bessie has bought her a coat and a cap,
  And started to wheel to the ball;
With only a bit of a skirt for a lap,
  And bloomers distressingly small!
Keep mourning, good Mother: your sobbings repeat;
For whether her going be tardy or fleet,
I never should know her, if her I should meet:
  We're lucky to catch her at all!

DE TEMPERACHEWER.

I'm an enterprisin' porter
  Of the Pennsylvani' Line;
An' I like it, an' I orter,
  Fur de business chance is fine;
But in journeys long or shorter,
  Dere is somethin' to endure;
An' de worst is, hearin', "Porter,
  Can't you change the temperachewer?"
An' I punch de little window,
  An' I pull it back an' forth,
For to satisfy the Hindoo,
  An' de people of de North.

Den a Texas Cuhnel want to
  Hab me closin' of de hole,
An' a parson from Toronto
  Say he's burnin' to a coal;
An' a maiden in a sorter
  Alto accent, sof' an' pure,
Chirrups up, an' warbles, "Porter,
  Caun't you change the temperachewer?"
An' I go an' fix de heater,
  Or pretend to, fur a while,
An' her darlin' face is sweeter,
  An' she tips me—(wid a smile).

Then a gentleman's on hand, w'ich
  Wants to take a Pullman fill,
An' an egg-cup an' a sandwich
  Nearly bu'sts a dollar-bill;
An' I think I'll reap a quarter;
  But de matter isn't sure,
Fur some fool 'll holler "Porter,
  Caun't you change the temperachewer?"
An' my man starts like a rocket,
  An' he shivers through an' through,
An' dat quarter in his pocket
  Sinks forevermore from view.

I suppose that some poor feller,
  In de various bye-an'-bye,
When de bad folks seek de cellar,
  An' de good is in de sky,
Some ol' sinful railroad sporter,
  Wid a burn he cannot cure,
Will be hollerin' "Porter! Porter!
  Caun't you change the temperachewer?"
Dey may press de knob—dose clippers—
  But no porter 'll do the rest;
We'll be brushin' golden slippers
  In de Pullmans of de blest.

ALWAYS A "KICK."

Farmer, how was your wheat this year?—
  Thrifty of stalk and head;
Plump of kernel and cleanly grown:
Better than any I ever have known:—
  The smiling farmer said.

How was your crop of corn this year,
  Marketed, floured, or fed?
Sleek and thick and yellow as gold,
And never a frost till the season was old:—
  The smiling farmer said.

How are your oats and barley and rye,
  Your apples of green and red?
How did the hay and potatoes thrive?
Never better since man was alive:—
  The candid farmer said.

Farmer, what was the guerdon you gained
  For crops that you marketed?
Prices stood at the very top,
And beckoned and beckoned for every crop:—
  The smiling farmer said.

Then you have nothing to grumble about,
  But praise and rejoice instead!—
Well, but then you must understand,
Such crops draw terribly on the land!
  The grumbling farmer said.

THE CONVICT AND THE STARS.

'Twas a cold clear winter evening, with the snow-wreaths drifted deep,
And a man whose hair was snow-white lay upon his couch asleep;
Lay in slumber sad and restless, as in talk with some one near
He could only see in glimpses, and could seldom feel or hear.
Not on down-upholstered pillows, or 'neath broidered counterpane,
Such as often grace the evening of a life of toil and gain;
Not mid walls of pictured splendor with the brush's memory rife;
Not mid textures from the fingers of a daughter or a wife;
But within a cell's close borders to be portioned, was his lot;
And the couch on which he rested was a dingy prison-cot.

Comes the clanging of a key-bolt—swings the door more grim than wide;
And the prison-surgeon marches to the wakened sufferer's side.
"You are ailing, they have told me. 'Tis the convict's usual song."
"I am ailing," said the old man, "but will not be, very long.
Will you listen to my story?" Then the calloused surgeon said:
"Of such matters I am weary; let me feel your pulse instead."
"I am innocent."—"Yes, maybe; that is e'er the pris'ner's creed;
I have never talked with convict, but some other did the deed."
"Nay, but listen! I have just heard one whose days were full of strife,
On his death-bed own the murder that has murdered all my life!
Yes, the law forbore to hang me, but it crucified instead;
It has nailed me to this prison, as it will till I am dead.
And tomorrow comes a 'pardon'; 'tis a way the statutes run,
That the Governor can forgive me for a crime I n'er have done.
Yes, tomorrow comes the 'pardon'; but 'twill enter over-late;
Long before 'tis here to seek me, I'll have passed the prison-gate."

Then the callous-hearted surgeon, holding still the prisoner's hand,
Said, "How you foretell this pardon, I can never understand.
How you know what now is passing at a bedside out of view,
Is a question; but I somehow feel the vision may be true!"
Then the convict said, "Pray, listen; I've a wife and children three;

They have passed the mystic bound'ries; they have gone ahead of me.
No great wonder that the villain who condemned me, I condemn;
For the sentence ere it killed me, used its power to murder them.
Sometimes, now, I see them plainly—then the darkness steps between;
And I doubt that I have viewed them, and my sorrow grows more keen.
Surgeon, may I ask a favor?—'tis the last I seek of you:
I would find a southern window, where the best stars are in view—
Those bright stars my wife and children conned with me, and loved so well—
Stars I have not seen for long years—from my grated prison-cell.
I have known such rank injustice—such perversions of God's right,
That I almost fear that God's stars have been blotted from the sight!"

"Take him to a southern chamber!"—stalwart men in stripes obeyed;
By a large and lofty window carefully the couch was laid.
"They are there!" he loudly shouted as they streamed into his sight;
And the prisoner in his gladness rose within the bed upright.
"There the evening star is gleaming, as it was serene and true,
When upon her father's doorstone oft we watched it out of view;
There the Pleiades are shining, as, when days of toil were done,
We oft wondered if God's palace was within that brightest one.
There Aldebaran is burning; oft my children used to cry,
'He is driving his gold harrow through the blue fields of the sky!'
Still the mighty wheels of Heaven draw the universe's cars;
Still I see the great Orion—mighty hunter—man of stars;
And the orb of orbs, proud Sirius, struggles up the hollow sky,
As he did when we were watching in the sweet days long gone by.
God is good! his laws are changeless; though oft hidden from our view,
Yet when bars and clouds have vanished, they flash out and gleam anew!

"Who are these that stand beside me?—who are these I feel and see?—
Wife and children, you are with me—you have come at last for me!
Farewell sorrow, pain, and misery; farewell bolts and prison-bars:
I am ready to go with you on your pathway 'mongst the stars!"

Stalwart men in stripes with reverence bore a body through the door;
On the morrow came the "pardon"; but release had come before.

NOTES.

"The Eclipse"—page 28. The total eclipse of the sun which occurred May 28, 1900, was one of the grandest spectacles ever presented in our stupendous panorama of the sky. No town within the belt of its influence, but turned out a good share of its population to watch the grand event. Industry throughout our country was for those few impressive minutes almost at a standstill, and the whole population became astronomers. It is singular that a thousand other grand phenomena—constantly taking place in the heavens, and foretold as surely as was this—are viewed by the great multitude of people, with entire indifference—or not noticed at all.

A story which I still roll as a very pleasant morsel under my tongue, is that of a fine old gentleman in Pennsylvania who had read, sixty years before, that the eclipse was to take place at a certain hour and minute. For the whole sixty years the question remained in his mind, as to whether the event would really take place as predicted by the votaries of science. Would the earth and sun both be exactly on time? Would not something happen, as so often with man's goings and comings, to prevent the accomplishment? Might not "the best laid plans" of the universe "gang a-gley"? Oh, if he could only live till the moment at which the eclipse was predicted!

He did. He journeyed into the belt of totality, and stood with watch in hand, on a bright, sunstrewn day, wondering if the prediction would come true.

It did: and he went home one of the happiest men on the earth.

"Funeral-Trains of Forest-Trees"—page 73. This line refers to the rafts of logs that are each season taken down the St. Lawrence River. They are very striking and picturesque, with broad expanses of fallen trees, lashed securely together, and suggesting great floating islands of wood.

"Then I sailed away a distance in my double-p'inted skift"—page 77. The St. Lawrence River skiff is pointed at both ends, and will run one way as well as the other. It is admirably adapted for rowing, sailing, fishing, or hunting; and no other kind would generally be seen upon that river, in a day's journey. The oarsman's dialect invariably refers to it as a "skift."

"An' my gracious them 'er fishes was a-eatin' cake an' pie!"—page 77. One fisherman whom the author remembers, used often to make this complaint: and on such occasions, would wait patiently till the fish became hungry again: when he generally succeeded in hauling them into his boat, in most approved style.

"Anyhow, the rich New Yorkers"—page 78. Not only New Yorkers, but people from other localities in different parts of the world, have been known to surreptitiously purchase fish, with which to make a good showing of their prowess when they returned to their homes or hotel, at night.

"Several things that Markham's fool"—page 80, refers to the poem, "The Man with the Hoe"—an admirably written, but deplorably misleading poem.

"To the Mountain Profile"—page 85. This magnificent freak of nature, famous everywhere as "The Old Man of the Mountain", is well known to those who have frequented the Franconia Range. It is situated twelve hundred feet above the vantage-ground, from which it is best viewed—the profile bearing an extraordinary resemblance to a human face (though not of the most refined character). The great rocks which compose it are forty feet from the top of the chin to the crown, and are wide in about the right proportion for a human face. The rock comprising forehead, mouth, and chin, are several feet apart: and there is no resemblance to the human face in a front view of them.

This great mountain-sculpture creates different impressions in different minds: and an attempt has been made in the two poems ("To the Mountain Profile" and "To the Same"), to depict the two extremes of these.

"Some Country Solace"—page 90. This poem was written "in the mind" one morning while in a hotel in the Catskill Mountains. The author was trying to get an early morning nap—and was cheated out of it by some of the sounds which he mentions.

"Shall I leave this man behind me in the hope to save my life?"—page 94. The author, having gone thus far, has always been unable to extricate the young people from their predicament, without drowning one or both of them. Several hundred sequels to the poem have been written by people in different parts of the country, suggesting various methods: but few of them were at all logical, or satisfactory.

"New England's Home-Call"—page 101. Within a few years, there has been quite generally adopted in the New England states, the beautiful custom of holding "Old Home Days"—in which a reunion is held, of residents, former residents, and descendants of the same.

"The Passing of the Mother"—page 106. This poem refers to Mrs. Mary A. Bickerdyke, generally known among the soldiers of our Civil War, as "Mother Bickerdyke." She was a wonderful combination of the sympathetic and the heroic, and was sincerely mourned by all who knew her and her wonderful history as a war-nurse.

"Gridley"—page 113. Captain Charles E. Gridley, Commander of Dewey's flagship, was noted as having fired the first shot in the great harbor-battle in

Manila. He died of a fever, soon after winning his honors. The author knew him from boyhood, and his struggles to reach the proud position that he held at the time of his death.

"Comin' Back to 'Pelier"—page 115. This was published and copied in newspapers throughout United States, several months before Admiral Dewey came home from his Manila triumph. The author had the privilege of seeing his prophecy fulfilled, and of witnessing the wonderful welcome given to the ocean-warrior at his home town, Montpelier, Vermont, on October 12, 1899.

"Colloquy of Grief"—page 122: written the next day after the death of our latest martyr-President—William McKinley.

"Liberty's Torch"—page 126: referring to the fact that the torch of Bartholdi's Statue of Liberty, in New York Harbor, was for several nights left unlighted, on account of the expense. This poem was published during that period. The light is now, the author is glad to say, beaming as brightly as ever.

"The Funeral-Express"—page 133. This was written upon a train running daily from Chicago to two cemeteries several miles outside the city. Several funerals are upon each train—the bodies all being placed in a special car, conveniently arranged with niches for that purpose. The daily excursion to these fields of the dead form a most impressive study, and the author has often accompanied them.

"To the Czar"—page 139. This was written in April, 1899, at the time Nicholas II. made an effort to have war abolished. It has not been recorded that he adopted the suggestion made in the last few lines.

"Song-bird in the dark"—page 142. For eighty-one years the renowned hymn-writer, Fanny Crosby, has been deprived of sight; and during most of that time, has been writing hymns, which are sung in every part of the civilized world.

THE END.

www.ingramcontent.com/pod-product-compliance
Lightning Source LLC
LaVergne TN
LVHW011238110826
845150LV00006B/1677

* 9 7 8 1 4 2 5 5 1 3 6 8 9 *